12 -
current

JOURNEYS
to the
MYTHICAL PAST

JOURNEYS
to the
MYTHICAL PAST

Book II of The Earth Chronicles Expeditions

ZECHARIA SITCHIN

Bear & Company
Rochester, Vermont

Bear & Company
One Park Street
Rochester, Vermont 05767
www.BearandCompanyBooks.com

Bear & Company is a division of Inner Traditions International

Library of Congress Cataloging-in-Publication Data
Sitchin, Zecharia.
    Journeys to the mythical past : book II of the Earth chronicles expeditions /
Zecharia Sitchin.
       p. cm.
    Summary: "The continuing autobiographical account of the investigations and
discoveries that led to The Earth Chronicles series"—Provided by publisher.
    ISBN-13: 978-1-59143-080-3
    ISBN-10: 1-59143-080-1
    1. Sitchin, Zecharia. 2. Archaeologists—Biography. 3. Civilization, Ancient. 4.
Civilization, Ancient—Extraterrestrial influences. I. Title. II. Title: Book II of the
Earth chronicles expeditions. III. Title: Earth chronicles expeditions.

    CC115.S58A3 2007
    930.1092—dc22
    [B]
                                                                    2007021955

Printed and bound in the United States by Lake Book Manufacturing

10 9 8 7 6 5 4 3 2

Text design and layout by Jon Desautels
This book was typeset in Garamond Pro with Herculanum used as a display typeface

Dedicated to my grandson
Ariel J. Feldman
who has beamed me up
to the Computer Age

CONTENTS

1   The Great Pyramid Forgery   1

2   Puzzling Cavities, Mysterious Sand   32

3   The Secret Chamber   52

4   The Fateful Day   62

5   OOPs in the Cairo Museum   75

6   Enigmas Made of Stone   91

7   The Iceman of the Alps   112

8   Insights to History   123

9   Vatican Encounters   135

10   Stargazers and Skymaps   154

11   Antikythera: A Computer Before Its Time   171

12   Nazca: Where the Gods Left Earth   190

     Postscript: Prophecies of the Return   214

1

THE GREAT PYRAMID FORGERY

The records of Egypt's archaeological finds include stories of varied bitter ends of the discoverer of this or the uncoverer of that, the most famed of which were the unusual deaths attributed to "King Tut's Curse" of those who had found his tomb; but I know of no such instance pertaining to probing the Great Pyramid and its mysteries. Even Agatha Christie's archaeological thrillers, that included murder on the Nile, did not take place inside the pyramid; and when James Bond was lured to Giza, the deathly encounter took place outside, near the Sphinx.

Ever since Napoleon, who invaded Egypt in 1798, made a visit to the Great Pyramid in Giza a tourist's "must," millions of people have entered it to admire, wonder, research and explore; yet I could not recall coming across even one report of a visitor's death inside it. **Thus, when I was almost killed there, I would have probably made a First . . .**

I was inside the Great Pyramid, at the top of the Grand Gallery, awaiting to climb up by a series of ladders into compartments above the King's Chamber, when I suddenly felt a mighty blow to my head: Someone had dropped from higher up a large and heavy piece of wood that knocked me down. Warm blood began to pour down from the top of my head, and I was certain that my skull had been cracked.

Though dazed and bleeding as I was rushed down and out, the

thoughts of death that raced through my mind included visions of newspaper headlines reporting my end. They ranged from an appropriate **Famous Author Killed Inside Great Pyramid,** to a humdrum **Visitor Dies in Giza Pyramid,** to—cursed was the thought—no headline at all. Upsetting was the headline **Fatal Tourist Accident in Egypt,** for I was certain that what had happened was no accident. And most disturbing was the imagined wisecracking headline **Curse of King Cheops?**—disturbing because I entered the pyramid that day to prove that the Pharaoh Cheops *did not* build the Great Pyramid.

Being able to write about the day when I was nearly killed in the Great Pyramid suggests that I managed to survive; but this is the very first time I am revealing what had happened. And as the reader can surely also guess by now, what happened that day had its origins, its beginning, long before. So, even before I tell the full story of that eventful and almost fatal day, it behooves me to backtrack to the Beginning.

***

There are many pyramids and pyramidical structures in Egypt, dotting the land from where the Nile River forms a delta in the north all the way south to ancient Nubia; the main ones are the twenty-odd pyramids (fig. 1) attributed to Pharaohs of the Old Kingdom (2650–2150 B.C.). These in turn consist of two distinct groups: The elaborately decorated pyramids associated with rulers of the Fifth and Sixth Dynasties (such as Unash, Teti, Pepi); and the pyramids ascribed to Third and Fourth Dynasty kings.

The later group's builders are clearly identified by a profusion of inscriptions on the pyramids' walls, the so-called Pyramid Texts; it is in regard to the earlier and paradoxically grander pyramids that the mysteries proliferate. With few written clues inside or beside them, or even entirely devoid of inscriptions or decorations, these earlier pyramids keep secret the mystery of their construction—Who built them and when, how were they built, and for what purpose. There are only theories and educated guesses.

Although no actual royal burial was ever discovered inside any

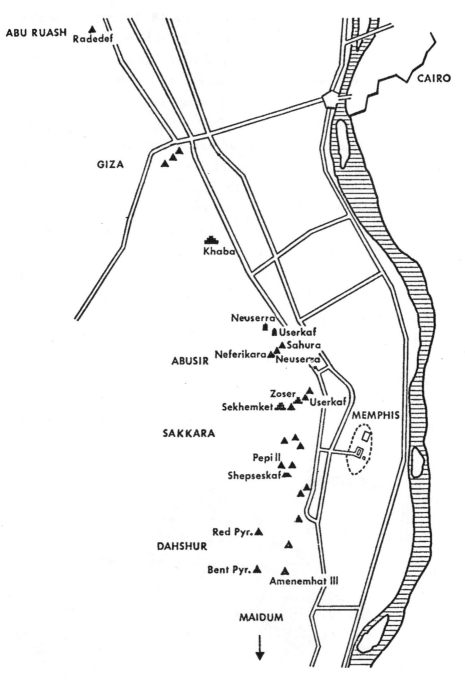

EGYPT: THE PRINCIPAL PYRAMID SITES

Figure 1

pyramid, the accepted theory has been that the pyramids were glorified royal tombs, evolving from the earlier flat horizontal *mastaba*—a large tombstone that covered the royal grave. Egyptologists assert that the first imposing pyramid, at Sakkara, belonged to king Zoser, the second Pharaoh of the Third Dynasty, whose ingenious architect piled up one mastaba on top another to create a **step pyramid** (fig. 2). The pyramid stands atop underground stone shafts, vaults, and passages decorated with carvings and blue-glazed tiles; we know it is Zoser's pyramid because some depictions of the king and inscriptions bearing his name were discovered there. The pyramid is surrounded by decorated stone structures and colonnades; but the pyramid itself, above ground, is poorly constructed with rough stones held in place by mud-clay mortar and tree stalks, all now exposed for the visitor to see. It is as though the above-ground and the below-ground parts of the pyramid were set apart, each following a different architectural and structural discipline.

Egyptologists hold that Zoser's Third Dynasty successors emulated him, on a lesser scale and with varied degrees of success, with step pyr-

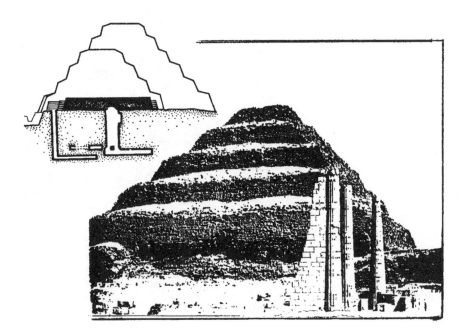

Figure 2

amids of their own; but then the last Pharaoh of the Third Dynasty, named Huni, decided to build a "true" pyramid with smooth sides, rising at the steep angle of 52°. It is known, appropriately, as the **Collapsed Pyramid,** for that attempt ended in dismal failure. What the visitor still sees at the site (at Maidum) is the step-shaped core surrounded by the debris of the collapsed masonry of the smooth-face mantle that the builders had attempted to attach to the core (fig. 3).

Why, all of a sudden, was an attempt made to shape this pyramid as a "true" pyramid, and where did the notion of a "true pyramid" with smooth triangular sides come from? Why was a steep angle of 52° chosen, and whether it was Huni—or, as some hold, his successor—who tried to attach the smooth mantle to the core, no one knows.

That successor was Sneferu, the first Pharaoh of the Fourth Dynasty. He was building (at Dahshur) his own "true" pyramid when the previous one, at Maidum, collapsed; so his architects (as plausibly held by some Egyptologists) abandoned the steep 52° angle in mid construction, and continued raising it at a flatter and much safer angle of 43°—resulting

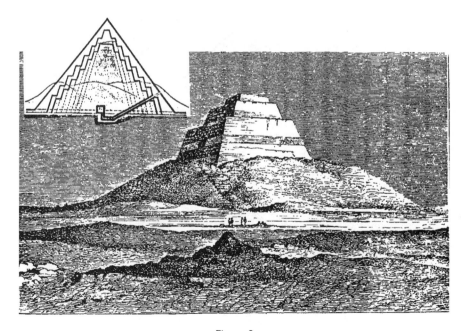

Figure 3

in what is known as the **Bent Pyramid** (fig. 4a); a stela (stone pillar) depicting the king and bearing Sneferu's name confirmed his association with this pyramid. Then Sneferu, still persisting in building a "true pyramid" with smooth sides, ordered the construction of a third pyramid (also at Dahshur). Known for the hue of its stones as the **Red Pyramid** (fig. 4b), it has the "correct" triangular sides rising from a square base and meeting at an apex. But its remains indicate that its sides rose at the safe angle of 44° . . .

And then—so Egyptological theories go—Sneferu's son and successor, a Pharaoh named *Khufu* (Cheops in English), managed to erect what is still the grandest stone edifice on Earth and the greatest of the "true" pyramids—the **Great Pyramid** of Giza. Dwarfing any previous pyramid in sheer size, it still rises like an artificial stone mountain at the magical angle of 52°—unique, majestic, unchallenged, and uncollapsed (plate 1).

Khufu's success—so the textbooks tell us—inspired his successors to build their pyramids next to his, at Giza. One, that outwardly emu-

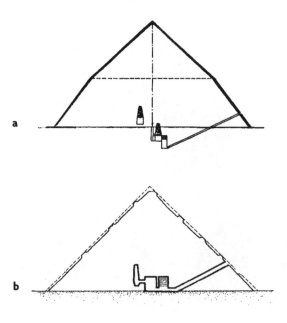

Figure 4

lates the Great Pyramid, was built by the Pharaoh **Chefra** (Chefren or Chephren in English), and is known as the **Second Pyramid**; because a causeway leads from it to the **Sphinx** (plate 2), it too is attributed to Chefra (although it stands much closer to the Great Pyramid). Then his successor, **Menkaura** (Mycerinus) built nearby the **Third Pyramid**— but for inexplicable reasons, as a miniature of the other two (fig. 5). Rising skyward where the desert stops at the Nile valley, the three, as the site map shows (fig. 6), were perfectly aligned to the cardinal points of the compass and to each other, forming an architectural unit as though they were planned by a single architect and not by three different Pharaohs separated by a century.

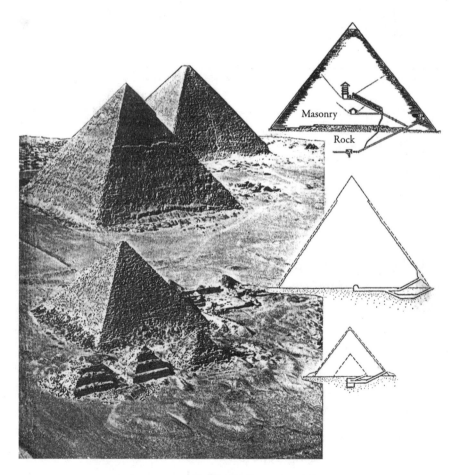

Figure 5

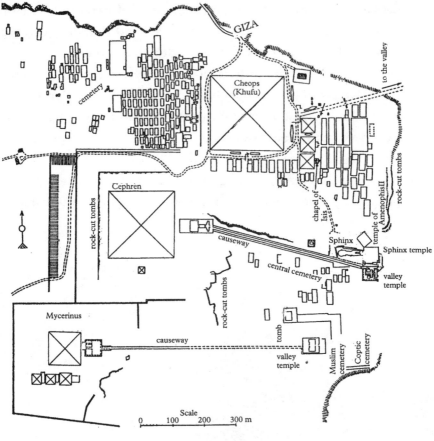

Figure 6

Unlike the other pyramids, the three Giza pyramids are devoid of any decorative feature, have no paintings or texts inscribed on their walls, hold no royal seal or effigy, and (with the exception to be discussed later) contain no other shred of evidence that the three were built by Khufu, Chefra, and Menkaura; Egyptologists nevertheless continue to adhere to their favorite theory of "pyramid per successive Pharaoh"—and they do so in regard to Giza even though the actual successor of Khufu was not Chefra but the Pharaoh Dedefra (also read Radedef) whose small crumbling pyramid, sloped at 48°, was built far away from Giza, at Abu Ruash in the north (see fig. 1, page 3).

The Egyptologists' list also conveniently omits two other Pharaohs who reigned between Chefra and Menkaura; and skipping a successor to the latter named Shepseskaf, continue the "pyramid age" straight into the Fifth Dynasty. Its first Pharaoh, Userkaf, built (at Abusir) a "true" pyramid at about half-size scale to that of the Great Pyramid of Giza. It adopted a slope angle similar to that of Giza; the result was a pile of rubble that even nowadays looks like a mud mound . . .

Next came a pyramid built by the Pharaoh Sahura, in Abusir. A much reduced-scale imitation of the great ones in Giza, it sloped at about 50°, and is also a pile of rubble now. So are the four built next, also in Abusir, by his successors Neferirkara, Raneferef, Neuserra, and Zedkara-Isesy. In and around the ruins, wall reliefs and other finds (including images of the kings and their hieroglyphic names) attest the extensive artworks and decorations in these pyramids and in their companion structures. But all that remains of the Fifth Dynasty century and a half of "true pyramid" building are piles of ruined rubble.

We now move with Egyptology to the profusely decorated and inscription-filled pyramids of the Sixth Dynasty. That part of the Pyramid Age began with the Pharaoh Unash (who some consider the last of the Fifth Dynasty rather than the first of the Sixth). He led the way back to Sakkara, in proximity to Zoser's step pyramid; adopting a one-third scale compared to Giza's Great Pyramid, he dared a slope akin to 52°—and ended up, like others before him, with a pile of rubble. The pyramids of the Sixth Dynasty Pharaohs who followed him in Sakkara—Teti, Pepi I, Mernera, Pepi II—ended up the same way. In spite of all the decorations and the verses from the Book of the Dead inscribed on their walls, the monuments that those Pharaohs had erected for their afterlife journeys to Eternal Life on the "Planet of Millions of Years" ended up as collapsed piles of rubble.

Having been to all these pyramids with their changed shapes and slope angles, and having seen their collapsed ruins—everywhere except in Giza, I could not accept without questioning the Egyptologists' assertion that the Giza pyramids *followed and emulated* the others. As I gazed at the remains of the other pyramids in the flat desert landscapes, my gut feeling was ***No—Giza was the example, the model that the others tried to emulate, and not vice versa!***

The Great Pyramid of Giza—in sheer size, in structural ingenuity and complexity, in mathematical and geometric precision, in enduring stability—has been unique, and there is no need here to illustrate that with well-known data; but that alone does not prove that it was the model for all the others. For that, the most compelling aspect is its inner *ascending* features. All the pyramids have inner features that are located in subterranean levels; but of all the pyramids (including its companions in Giza—fig. 7 compares the main ones in size and inner complexity)— *the Great Pyramid is the only one with ascending passages and complex inner components high above ground level.*

The story of the discovery of those ascending and upper inner features is a key to understanding the true sequence of pyramid construction in Egypt; the mystery of the plugging off of the ascending features is a clue to the true identity of the Giza builders.

***

The Giza pyramids as seen nowadays are without the smooth white limestone facing they originally had—the handiwork of robbers who stripped off the valuable limestones for use in neighboring Cairo and surrounding villages. In the Second Pyramid, the strippers fell short of the uppermost courses and the limestone "skin" can still be seen only way up; in the Great Pyramid some of the facing stones remained at the base, serving to indicate the precise slope angle (fig. 8). Today's visitor enters the Great Pyramid by climbing up several courses of the stone blocks of its exposed masonry, and goes through a forced opening in the pyramid's north face that leads to its innards via a tunnel-like passage. However, as one looks at the pyramid while still outside (fig. 9), it becomes obvious that this entrance lies somewhat lower and sideways than the true original entrance, which is marked by two sets of massive stone slabs touching diagonally to protect the entranceway (fig. 10a, page 14). There, when the pyramid still had its smooth facing, a swivel stone not only shut the entrance but also hid it completely from an outside onlooker (fig. 10b).

That such an original entranceway, with its swivel stone, had existed was not a complete secret in antiquity; though hidden from view, Egyp-

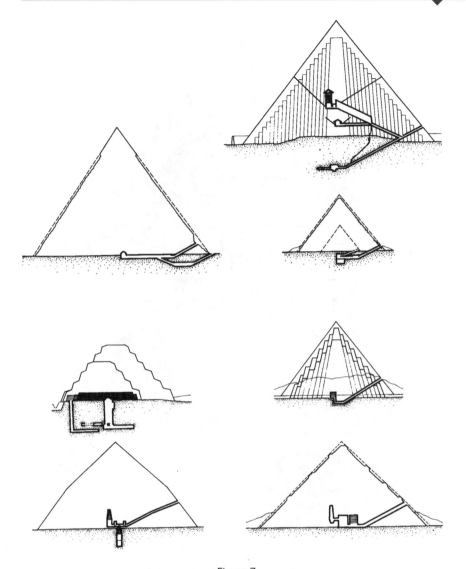

Figure 7

tian priests knew of it. In fact Strabo, the first century A.D. Roman geographer and historian, reported that when he visited Egypt he entered the Great Pyramid through an opening in the north face hidden by a "hinged stone," and went down a long and narrow passage all the way to a pit dug in the bedrock—just as other Roman and Greek visitors had done before him.

Example of the Casing-Stones of a Pyramid, Super-Posed.
On the rect-angular masonry courses. From a photograph by P. S. of the Summit of the 27 pyr.

Remnant of the Original Casing-Stone Surface of the Great Pyramid.
Near the middle of its northern foot. As dicovered by the excavation of Col. Howard Vyse in 1857.

Figure 8

But as the centuries went by, and Egyptian priests gave way to Christian monks and then Moslem clerics, the exact location of this hidden entranceway was forgotten. In A.D. 820, when the Moslem caliph Al Mamoon sought to enter the pyramid to find its rumored Chamber of Treasures, his engineers and masons ended up hacking their way in—

Figure 9

correctly in the north face, but somewhat below the right spot. Their forced opening is the entrance through which today's visitor goes in.

Once inside, all that Al Mamoon's men found were stone blocks and more stone blocks. Hammering and chiseling, they cracked their way in by alternately heating and cooling the mass of stones. Finally, they reached a narrow inclined passageway; it led all the way down, through masonry and then bedrock, to an empty pit—*the very same descending passage and pit described by Strabo.*

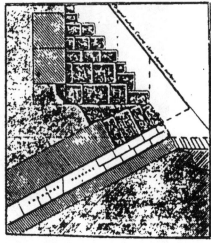

a   b

Figure 10

The passageway also led up; following it for a short distance, Al Mamoon's men found the original entrance from the inside. Were the story to end there, Al Mamoon's efforts would have only confirmed what was known and believed in previous Roman, Greek, and prior Egyptian times: that the Great Pyramid, as its two companions and all the other pyramids, had only an inner *descending* passage and below ground-level features (fig. 11a).

The secret that the Great Pyramid, alone of all the pyramids, also had amazing upper passages and chambers would have remained unknown were it not for an accidental discovery by Al Mamoon's men. As they went on ramming and blasting, they suddenly heard a loosened stone fall. Searching in the direction of the sound, they found that a fallen triangular stone had hidden from view blocking granite slabs emplaced diagonally to the passage. Unable to break it or move it, they tunneled around it—and reached what is now known as the *Ascending Passage* (fig. 11b). It led up through the "Grand Gallery" via a horizontal passage to the "Queen's Chamber" and farther up to the "King's Chamber" (fig. 11c). The amazing and unique inner upper complexities of the Great Pyramid were discovered.

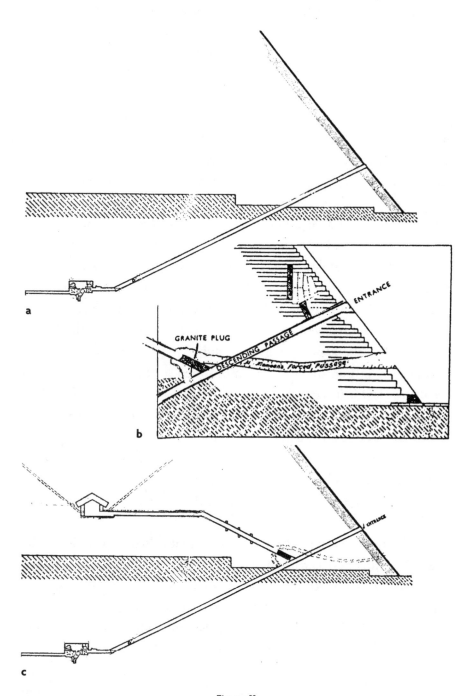

Figure 11

Pyramid researchers now recognize that at some point in time after the Great Pyramid was built, "someone" for "some reason" slid down a grooved channel in the Ascending Passage three granite plug-stones that sealed off completely all the upper inner parts of the pyramid, and hid them so well from sight that anyone entering the pyramid through its proper entranceway would only know of the Descending Passage. The inner upper parts became permanently sealed and forever hidden. That is why, I have explained, all the other Egyptian pyramids from Zoser's on had only descending passages and compartments; for all of them emulated the Great Pyramid *as they knew it,* and as its companions at Giza suggested: Only descending passages and inner parts below ground level.

How, when, and why was the upper passageway sealed? The best (or only) idea Egyptologists have is that the sealing-off took place after the Pharaoh's burial in the "coffer" in the "King's Chamber" was completed. But when Al Mamoon finally broke into the upper passages and chambers, the coffer was empty and no one was buried in the King's Chamber. No, the granite plugs were slid down, I wrote, when the god Ra/Marduk, in punishment, was imprisoned in the Great Pyramid to die a slow death. It happened during what I have termed in *The Wars of Gods and Men* as the **Pyramid Wars—*when gods, not men, ruled Egypt,*** long before any Pharaonic dynasties.

This finding alone should suffice for concluding that the Giza pyramids had been built before all the other pyramids in Egypt were erected; but there is more compelling evidence that leads to that unavoidable conclusion.

Such evidence can start with showing that a "true" pyramid, as the Great Pyramid of Giza, had existed—and was known and even depicted long before Zoser or Khufu and their dynasties. One can submit in evidence a well-known ancient Egyptian artifact called the *Victory Tablet of King Menes* (also known as the Narmer Palette), who was the first king of the very first dynasty. It shows on one side the king wearing the white crown of Upper Egypt, defeating its chieftains and conquering their cities. On the tablet's other side Menes is shown wearing the red crown of Lower Egypt—where Giza is situated; and there the pictographic symbols most clearly include a smooth-sided triangular "true" pyramid (fig. 12), indicating that such a pyramid had already been known circa 3100 B.C.—half a millennium before Cheops/Khufu.

Indeed, inscriptions (fig. 13) on a stone artifact belonging to Cheops—in which his name Khufu is clearly written in hieroglyphics—

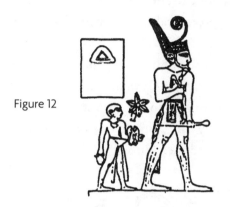

Figure 12

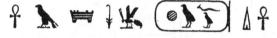

Ankh	Hor	Mezdau	Suten-bat	Khufu	tu ankh
Live Horus Mezdau;			(To) King (of)	Khufu, is given Life!

Upper & Lower Egypt,

The common opening, invoking Horus and proclaiming long life for the king, then packs explosive statements:

He founded	the House	of Isis,	Mistress of the Pyramid,

beside the House of the Sphinx

Figure 13

imply that *the Great Pyramid had already existed in his time, and so did the Sphinx!* In this monument, known as the **Inventory Stela,** Khufu took credit for restoring a shrine to the goddess Isis, "Mistress of the Pyramid." He does not take credit for the pyramid itself, clearly considering it a structure belonging to gods, not mortals; and he states that the shrine stood "beside the house of the Sphinx"—the very Sphinx which according to Egyptological tenets was erected (or carved out) by Khufu's *successor* Chefra . . .

In fact, depictions of the Sphinx (as reported by Sir W. M. Flinders Petrie in *The Royal Tombs of the Earliest Dynasties,* 1901) were already found on stone tablets belonging to the earliest Pharaohs Menes-Narmer and Zer (fig. 14). Clearly, the Sphinx too had already existed when Khufu and Chefra ascended their thrones.

Figure 14

If the Giza pyramids (and the Sphinx) had already existed when Pharaohs began to reign, who was there to build them? The answer comes to us from the Near East's earliest civilization, that of Sumer. The Sumerians were quite aware of the unique edifices at Giza, describing them in texts dealing with the Pyramid Wars and depicting them on cylinder seals (fig. 15a), including one commemorating the victory of the god Ninurta by showing his Divine Eagle surmounting the two large pyramids (fig. 15b).

***

The story of the "Pyramid Wars" is told in *The Wars of Gods and Men*. The story of how the Giza pyramids and Sphinx came to be built, by the gods, as vital components of their post-Diluvial Spaceport, has been told in my book *The Stairway to Heaven*.

Gods, not men, built the Giza pyramids as terminals for the Landing Corridor that was anchored on the twin peaks of Ararat in the north and on two natural peaks in the Sinai peninsula in the southeast

Figure 15

(fig. 16); absent such peaks at the northeastern terminus, the gods first erected the small pyramid as a test of structural stability and functionality, then built the other larger two—equipping the Great Pyramid with pulsating guidance equipment in the unique upper innards.

We can even explain the difficult slope angle of 52° by the fact that it was the "secret number" of the Divine Architect, Thoth (whom the Sumerians called Ningishzidda)—a number that linked the Great

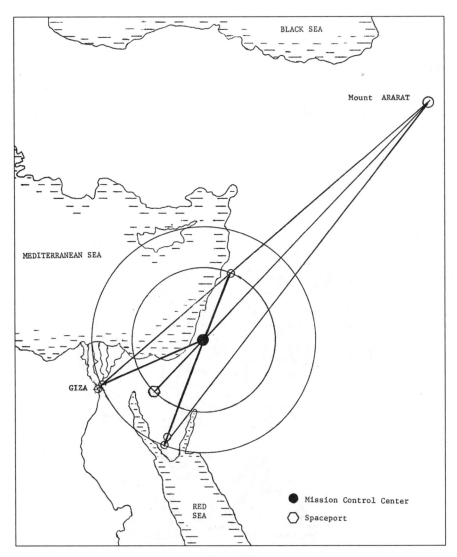

Figure 16

Pyramid's base length and height to a circle's π. Yet with all that, Egyptologists have remained unmovable in the Khufu-Chefra-Menkaura sequence. How and when did this tenet originate?

Spending weeks at a time in the British Museum Library in London, poring over countless books on the subject backward—from the latest to the earliest, I found that all the textbooks reported that Herodotus, the Greek historian-geographer, was told so by his guides when he visited Egypt in the fifth century B.C. Some textbooks asserted that the royal name of Khufu was actually found inscribed within the Great Pyramid; they also used to state that a coffin lid bearing the name "Menkaura" was discovered inside the Third Pyramid. Could anyone argue with that?

The fact that later textbooks ceased referring to the information, given in earlier books, about the Menkaura coffin lid intrigued me. Why was such physical evidence no longer mentioned? Searching for an answer in issues of scholarly journals, I unearthed the whole story. The original find, of the coffin lid and skeletal remains of the Pharaoh, was made in 1837 by two Englishmen who resifted debris inside the Third Pyramid. Textbooks accepted this as proof of the pyramid builder's identity for more than a century—until modern carbon dating methods established that the coffin lid was not from 2600 B.C. but from circa 660 B.C. (when a later Pharaoh also called himself Menkaura), and the skeletal remains from the first or second century A.D.

The 1837 "find" was therefore dropped from textbooks (and the British Museum removed the coffin lid from its catalogue); but the circumstances intrigued me. Why did all previous explorers inside this small pyramid miss the remarkable physical evidence? Also, since the lid and the skeletal remains were from totally different periods, how did they happen to rest together? Did the "finders" perpetrate a deliberate archaeological fraud? Their names, I learned, were Howard Vyse and John Perring; they were quite a team, excavating almost at will in Giza. Then, joined by a wheeler-dealer named J. R. Hill, it was the same Howard Vyse who discovered the name "Khufu" written inside the Great Pyramid, where—you guessed it—none was found before . . .

That realization, that an archaeological fraud was perpetrated in the small Third Pyramid, launched me on a course that led to question the only "proof" of the Khufu-built-it tenet of Egyptology.

Howard Vyse was a retired British colonel, a "black sheep" of a wealthy family, who, visiting Egypt in 1835, became infatuated with Egyptian antiquities. Though the Firman (exploration permit) that was issued to Vyse by the Egyptian authorities named the British Consul in Cairo (a Col. Campbell) as a trustee, Vyse made his own hiring decisions; and in Giza he entrusted the search to one Battista Caviglia, who made important finds at the Sphinx and assured Vyse that discovering the elusive hidden Treasure Chamber in the Great Pyramid was just a matter of time and money. Vyse provided the money and left Egypt to tour the Levant. He returned two years later, only to be told that the search had led nowhere. Starting to run out of both money and time, Vyse took matters into his own hands, moved to Giza, and enlisted a mix of helpers—some with Egyptological experience (such as C. Sloane and J. Perring), and some local wheeler-dealers (a Mr. Hill, a Mr. Mash, a Mr. Raven).

A detailed day-by-day diary that he kept (later published as *Operations Carried On at the Pyramids of Gizeh*) records the desperation as nothing worthwhile was found. The British Consul and other dignitaries started to visit the site, wondering where the efforts were leading. One of the problems was the need to constantly find new workmen, since those hired developed eyesores as they hacked and hammered inside the dust-filled pyramid; it got so bad that, on Col. Campbell's intervention, the British sent a team to build an eye hospital in Giza. As the year 1837 began and his funds were running out, the frustrated Vyse started to use gunpowder in order to blast his way *inside* the Great Pyramid; he hired an English stonemason, who had come to Egypt for the eye hospital project, to handle the detonations.

His last resort were narrow spaces above the King's Chamber, one of which ("Davison's Chamber") was discovered by Nathaniel Davison in 1765. The gunpowder blasts revealed that there was a cavity above Davison's Chamber; forcing his way up, Vyse discovered a similar space above Davison's. Like Davison's, it was totally devoid of any decoration or inscription. Vyse named it Wellington's Chamber in honor of his favorite war hero, and had his assistant Hill inscribe this name inside the narrow chamber with red paint. Continuing the use of gunpowder as his men moved farther up, Vyse discovered two more similar empty spaces; he named them in honor of Lord Nelson and Lady Arbuthnot—names recorded by Mr. Hill in the usual red paint. Then he reached the vaulted cavity at the top, naming it Campbell's Chamber in honor of his consular patron.

All the "chambers of construction" (as he called them—they are now called "Relieving Chambers") were bare and empty—no Pharaonic remains, no treasure—just black dust on the uneven floors. But on re-entering the chambers (Mr. Hill, Mr. Perring, Mr. Mash kept going in), "quarry marks" in red paint were noticed (fig. 17).

It was in those days of despair and desperation that a major discovery was made that assured Vyse's place in the annals of Egyptology: Among the quarry marks were several cartouches that spelled out royal names, including that of Khufu! (fig. 18a, b)

The British and Austrian consuls in Cairo were invited to witness the discovery; Mr. Hill copied the inscriptions on parchment sheets, and all present authenticated them with their signatures. The documents were then sent to the British Museum in London, and the unprecedented discovery was announced for the whole world to know. Since no one had entered those upper chambers from the time when the pyramid was erected, here was unchallenged proof of its builder's name!

Vyse's find has remained the only evidence for the Khufu–Great Pyramid connection. But while textbooks state so unquestioningly, it appears that at the time, experts (including the British Museum's Samuel Birch and the great German Egyptologist Karl Richard Lepsius) were uneasy about the inscriptions' script—it was one that was introduced in ancient Egypt much later—and questioned whether they really spelled out correctly the name Khufu (it looked like two different royal names were actually inscribed).

As I was poring over Vyse's printed diary, something odd struck me:

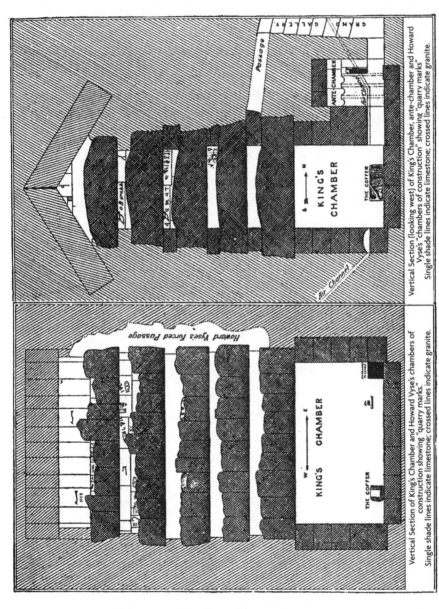

Looking North

Vertical Section of King's Chamber and Howard Vyse's chambers of construction showing "quarry marks."
Single shade lines indicate limestone; crossed lines indicate granite.

Looking West

Vertical Section (looking west) of King's Chamber, ante-chamber and Howard Vyse's "chambers of construction" showing "quarry marks."
Single shade lines indicate limestone; crossed lines indicate granite.

Figure 17

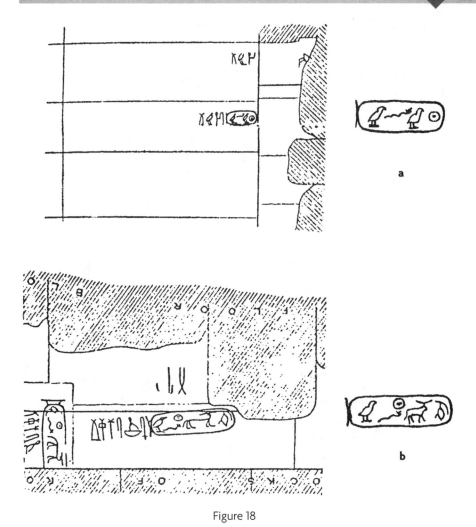

Figure 18

The royal name he showed was inscribed differently than on the Inventory Stela; instead of diagonal lines (a "sieve") inside a circle which reads KH (and thus KH-U-F-U), Vyse's finds were written with a circle with just a dot inside (fig. 19). That reads not KH but RA, the sacred name of Egypt's supreme god. **Thus, the name Vyse reported was not KHufu, but RA-u-f-u . . .**

In 1978, visiting the British Museum, I asked to see the Vyse parchments. It took some doing, as no one had asked for them as far as anyone could recall. But the *Hill Facsimiles* (as they were catalogued) were

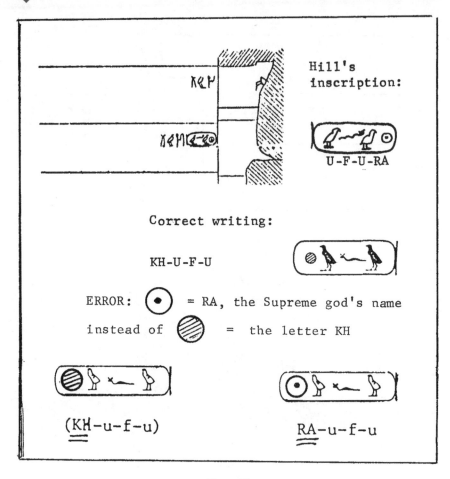

Figure 19

found and shown to me—a bundle tied with yellowing-white ribbon. The authenticated parchments were there, the way they reached the museum more than a century earlier; **and the misspelling was also there:** In no instance was the "Kh" inscribed correctly as a sieve with diagonal lines; instead there was a dot or a smudge inside a circle, spelling "Ra." Could it be that someone, in antiquity, had used the name of the great god RA in vain—an unforgivable sacrilege, a blasphemy punishable by death?

As I read the diary entries again, the words *"red paint"* kept jumping out of the pages—as when Mr. Hill used it to inscribe the names "Lord

Wellington," "Lady Arbuthnot," "Lord Nelson." I was struck by a statement in Perring's own memoirs *(The Pyramids of Gizeh)* that the red paint used for the ancient inscriptions "was a composition of red ochre called by the Arabs *moghrah* **which is still in use.**" Then Perring added the observation on the paint's quality: "Such is the state of preservation of the marks in the quarries that **it is difficult to distinguish the work of yesterday from one of three thousand years**" (emphasis mine). Was he voicing his own astonishment about how fresh the red paint markings looked—*after 4,500 years!*—or was he offering an explanation for the odd phenomenon?

As I went back to Vyse's day-by-day diaries, the entries made clear that the "quarry marks" (as Vyse called them) *were not discovered when the chambers were first entered;* and that it was Mr. Hill or Mr. Perring—not Vyse himself—who were first to notice the red-paint markings on subsequent visits. And then the thought struck me: Could the team that perpetrated the fraud in the Third Pyramid have also engaged in a forgery inside the Great Pyramid—"discovering" inscriptions where absolutely none have been found before?

Wasn't it odd, I thought, that for centuries no markings *of any kind* were found by *anyone, anywhere,* in the pyramid, not even in Davison's Chamber above the King's Chamber—and only Vyse found such markings *where only he first entered?*

Based on Vyse's own diary entries, the accusing finger pointed to Mr. Hill as the culprit, and I suggested that it was on the night of May 28, 1837, that he entered the pyramid with brush and red paint and simulated the royal name. The Great Pyramid Discovery was a great fraud, an archaeological forgery.

***

Without the "Khufu" inscription, Egyptologists remain without any tangible evidence for naming him as the builder of the Great Pyramid—and for that matter of Chefra and Menkaura as the builders of the two other Giza pyramids. The evidence that *does exist* shows that these pyramids and the Sphinx had preceded the Pharaohs; and the only ones who were there millennia earlier, who had the technology, who had the reason for erecting these pyramids—were the Anunnaki.

Convinced that that is what had happened, I detailed the evidence in my 1980 book *The Stairway to Heaven*.

The forgery conclusion caused a minor sensation. Several dailies (among them the *Washington Times,* the *Pittsburgh Press*) and magazines picked up the story, some even at length, some even embellishing the report with a cartoon (fig. 20). There were radio interviews. But the Egyptological community ignored it—and it took me awhile to understand why: It was one thing to suggest that a questionable inscription was a forgery; it was quite another thing to expect Egyptologists to acknowledge that the pyramids were built by "Extraterrestrials" . . .

***

In May 1983, three years after *The Stairway to Heaven* was published, I received an astonishing letter. It was from a Mr. Walter M. Allen of Pittsburgh, Pa. "I have read your book," he wrote. "What you say about the forgery in the Cheops Pyramid was not new to me." His great-grandfather, he wrote, **was an eyewitness to the forgery!**

Figure 20

"I have your letter of May 7th and am literally flabbergasted," I wrote him back. "That my conclusion could be supported by a virtual eyewitness was beyond my wildest expectations!"

As the story unfolded, it turned out that Mr. Allen's great-grandfather, Humphries W. Brewer, was the very stonemason from England whom Col. Vyse had hired. A civil engineer and master mason, he came to Egypt to assist a Dr. Naylor who was building an eye hospital for the local workmen. When the project was discontinued, Humphries was hired by Vyse to supervise the blasting inside the pyramid. He used to write regularly home, describing to his father back in Wiltshire, England, what was happening in Giza. In one of the letters he gave his family the sad news that he was dismissed from his job, and told how and why: *He witnessed Mr. Hill go into the pyramid with red paint and brush, supposedly to paint over ancient markings, but actually to paint new ones.* When the young stonemason objected, he was fired and banned from the site. "He did not get along with Perring and Raven because of the events . . . he trusted the judgment of Caviglia and Col. Campbell," Mr. Allen added in his letter. He signed it "Walter M. Allen, AFTER 150 YEARS" (capital letters his own).

How did he know all that? In 1848 the family moved from England to the United States, settling in upstate New York; they brought with them family records and memorabilia, including Humphries Brewer's letters from Egypt. In the 1950s Mr. Allen, realizing time was running out, started to visit family elders still living, recording what they recalled about the family's history. The sources included his mother, two daughters of Humphries (Mary Brewer Christie and Rebecca Brewer Allen), an aunt Nell, an uncle Col. Jos Walker, M.D. A radio buff, Mr. Allen used the empty pages in his radio logbook to write down what they said. Some of the recollections turned to the time his great-grandfather was in Egypt, hired to use gunpowder inside the Great Pyramid, and what he had witnessed.

I asked Mr. Allen for any documentary evidence he had. He said that he would ask around for the letters, but would send me in the meantime photocopies of his logbook entries, which he did.

An entry dated Sat. Oct. 9, 1954 (fig. 21—*here made public for the first time*) recorded a conversation with his mother and refers to a visit with Nell Pattington in Corning, N.Y., who "had some of Humfreys letters & Wm. Brewers letters from England. Got them from her father Wm. Marchant Brewer." The entry included the following:

Humfrey received prize for bridge he designed in Vienna over Danube. H. went to Egypt 1837, British Medical Serv. to Egypt ... They were to build hospital in Cairo for Arabs with severe eye afflictions. Dr. Naylor took Humfrey along. Treatment not successful, hospital not built. He joined a Col. Visse exploring Gizeh pyramids. Rechecked dimensions 2 pyramids. Had dispute with Raven and Hill about painted marks in pyramid. Faint marks were repainted, some were new ... Humfrey went to Syria & Jerusalem to see holy city few weeks later. Had words with a Mr. Hill and Visse when he left. He agreed with a Col. Colin Campbell & another Geno Cabilia. Humfrey went back to England late 1837.

I felt a chill when I read these lines. Written in 1954—more than twenty years *before* my book was published—they resurrected the players of the 1837 drama: Vyse, Campbell, Caviglia, Hill, Raven, Dr. Naylor—and clearly identified the culprits as Hill and Raven.

Other entries, and a letter from an uncle, confirmed the basic facts regarding Humphries Brewer, who he was, his time in Egypt, his dispute with "Visse and Hill," and his banishment from Giza, adding a tidbit that the German Egyptologist Richard Karl Lepsius invited Humphries to join him when he wanted to examine the "marks" inside the pyramid—but both were refused permission by Vyse.

Though Mr. Allen's search for the bundle of Humphries' letters was unsuccessful, the above quoted lines remain an authentic, unbiased eyewitness testament to what had happened: *"Paint marks were repainted, some were new."*

Some months after the above exchanges with Mr. Allen, I was invited to be interviewed (via long-distance phone) on a talk show on a Pitts-

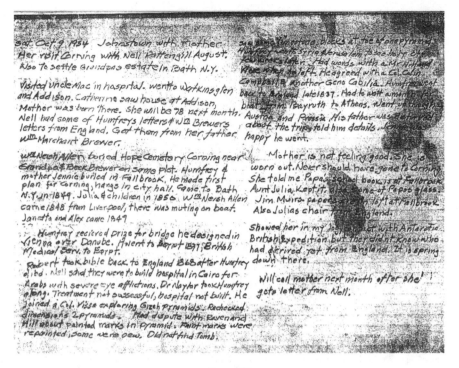

Figure 21

burgh radio station. As the interview turned to the pyramid forgery, the host said: I have a surprise for you—we have Mr. Walter Allen in the studio!

Continuing the interview with both of us, the host asked Mr. Allen to restate the facts that I described as *he* knew them—and he did. No doubt was left: **The forgery in the Great Pyramid was confirmed by an eyewitness.**

In spite of a segment in the TV program *Ancient Mysteries,* more articles, and references to the forgery evidence in several books by non-academics, no headway was made in Establishment circles. But my persistent curiosity—or was it Fate?—did not let the matter rest there.

2

PUZZLING CAVITIES, MYSTERIOUS SAND

As readers of my writings know, it has been my aim to actually visit the places I was writing about; and with the exception of Iraq under Saddam Hussein, I have by and large done so. I have of course been to Egypt and the Sinai peninsula—locations of the pyramids, the Sphinx, and Mount Sinai, of which I wrote in *The Stairway to Heaven.* Now the eyewitness evidence provided by Mr. Allen prompted me to find a way to also visit the "crime scene"—to get inside the Great Pyramid and the Relieving Chambers where the red paint markings were.

That, I knew, was then almost as impossible as my other ambition: To obtain a helicopter with which to land on the true Mount Sinai; but I was determined to do it.

I began the preparations as soon as *The Stairway to Heaven* was published. Through the Egyptian Ambassador in Washington copies of the book, accompanied by proper letters of recommendation, were sent to President Anwar Sadat of Egypt and other VIPs there. In addition to this political high-level channel, I tried to smooth the way to the necessary permissions on an "operative" (i.e., bureaucratic) level: I became a member of the influential American Research Center in Egypt (ARCE), and was personally introduced to Dr. Mohamed Ibrahim Bakr, Chairman of the Egyptian Antiquities Organization that controlled all such matters. With the way to success thus smoothed, I went to Egypt in 1982. In Cairo, some of the VIPs on my list were not there—starting with President Sadat, who had been assassinated the previous October. Of those in town, everyone was nice and hospitable; but none of the high-level connections led anywhere.

I did not give up. After the attempt in 1982, I found what I thought might be a more practical avenue. As many who have made repeat visits to the Great Pyramid have found out, the actual on-site control is in the hands of the robed guards/guides stationed at the entrance who can let you in when the Pyramid is officially closed, or open for you a locked chamber "by arrangement." As my luck would have it, the very boss of all the Giza guardians was right here in the USA—completing his graduate studies at the University of Pennsylvania in Philadelphia. His name was Zahi Hawass; his title was Chief Inspector of the Giza Pyramids; and he was giving a lecture at the University Museum (of which I was a member). I attended and introduced myself to the speaker. I told him about my books; he indicated to me his interest in giving lectures, and in finding a publisher for a book that he was writing; I offered to be of help. I also found out there that he was going to lead an "Egypt in Depth" tour in September/October 1984 (fig. 22).

I not only enrolled myself and my wife in the tour—I also sent Mr. Hawass copies of *The 12th Planet* and *The Stairway to Heaven* with a nice letter describing my interest in Egypt's antiquities. The tour, however, was canceled; so I called Mr. Hawass and told him I was ready to go on my own—if he could arrange for me to go into the Great Pyramid and see the Relieving Chambers. In response, Mr. Hawass provided me with a letter of introduction addressed to "Mr. Ahmed Mousa, Director of Antiquities at the Giza plateau," asking him to enable the bearer of the letter "to see whatever he wants to see in Giza."

Before leaving for Egypt in November 1984, I made a photocopy of the letter for my files (fig. 23); I have kept it all these years as a significant memento, because, as time went on, Dr. Zahi Hawass moved up the antiquities hierarchy to become the virtual dictator in all matters

Egypt in Depth Tour
With Chief Inspector of
Giza Pyramids

Escorted by:
Zahi Hawass
Chief Inspector of the Giza Pyramids
September 29-October 15, 1984
March 09-March 25, 1985

Figure 22

THE UNIVERSITY MUSEUM
of Archaeology/Anthropology

University of Pennsylvania   33rd and Spruce Streets   Philadelphia, PA 19104   (215) 898-4000

Figure 23

concerning Giza and other Egyptian antiquities—and because our paths were fated to cross again, *including on that fateful day in 1997 when I was almost killed inside the Great Pyramid.*

I arrived in Giza with the all-important letter to Mr. Ahmed Mousa full of expectations; disappointment was not late in coming . . . Benefiting from experience, I first went to the pyramid's entrance, to find out what was going on, what can be seen, what can be entered—by

private arrangement, if necessary. There was no way to reach the Relieving Chambers, they said; climbable scaffolding needs to be erected for
that. I went to the office building that stands on a rise to the right of
the pyramid plaza. Mr. Mousa, I was told, was away. His assistant, a Mr.
Ibrahim, took the letter and promised I'd be called at my hotel; I knew
there was a fat chance for that, so I was back at the Director's office the
next day, waiting and waiting for Mr. Ibrahim to show up. When he did,
I was told that they are working on my request, but *really* there is no way
to climb up where I want to go; higher up permissions are needed to set
up access; it'll take time; I have to be patient . . . I spent the day poking
in and around the Pyramids and Sphinx; I spent a day in the Egyptian
Museum; I hired a driver and went to explore Sakkara. For five days
there was no news. I went back to New York.

***

Unbeknown to me at the time, my conclusion that the Great Pyramid
and its companions in Giza (the two other pyramids and the Sphinx)
were thousands of years older than Khufu's time did not go unnoticed
in Virginia Beach, Va., where the Association for Research and Enlight-
enment has been headquartered. The A.R.E. promotes and teaches the
legacy of the famed "Seer" Edgar Cayce, whose wide-ranging "readings"
decades earlier included visions of the past. He spoke repeatedly of a lost
civilization that preceded the Pharaohs in Egypt, and credited it with
building the Great Pyramid and the Sphinx. The date? 10500 B.C.—the
very date of my conclusions!

In 1985 the A.R.E. sent a team to Giza to verify Cayce's predictive
date through newly developed carbon dating techniques. Samples of
organic matter (wood, charcoal) that somehow got stuck on the pyramid's stone blocks were collected and sent for dating to two highly
reputable laboratories. The samples from the Great Pyramid were found
to range in age from about 2900 B.C. (give or take 100 years) *for material collected from its bottom* to 3800 B.C. (plus or minus 160 years) *for
samples from the topmost courses.* The dates were far from 10500 B.C., yet

they predated Khufu from several centuries to more than twelve hundred years.

The investigators confirmed that no samples were collected inside the pyramid; all were from the exterior—organic material stuck to the stone blocks *when they were exposed*. This could happen either *before* the limestone casing was installed, or *after* it was ripped off. Because of the dating results, to assume the former required the pyramid to have been built upside down, first the topmost courses (samples dated 3800 B.C.) and then the lower ones (samples dated 2900 B.C.). To assume the latter meant that the limestone casing *was already gone centuries before Khufu's time*. I was invited by the A.R.E. for my comments; they were published as a featured cover article in its journal *Venture Inward* (November/December 1986 issue).

(The enigma of the disappeared limestone casing stones has never been satisfactorily explained by Egyptologists; the conjecture—that the large, precisely shaped and angled blocks were ripped off for use in local construction—fails to show where the huge number of these blocks had gone; hardly any have been found in Cairo or surrounding villages. The true answer might be that they were destroyed during the "Pyramid Wars," as described in my book *The Wars of Gods and Men*.)

My suggestion that the Giza complex was built circa 10500 B.C. was also getting "celestial corroboration," in a manner of speaking. As it turned out, two British authors (Robert Bauval and Adrian Gilbert) were researching at that time their idea that the Giza layout (see fig. 6, page 8) emulated the celestial layout of the Orion constellation and its stars. Their problem was that (due to the phenomenon of Precession) the Giza layout seems to emulate the Orion layout as it had been not in Khufu's time but thousands of years earlier. Not wishing to challenge Egyptological chronology head on, the two authors (in their book *The Orion Mystery*) said that even if the Pharaohs did build the pyramids, the Giza layout followed a ***"prior alignment with Orion—in 10490 B.C."***

But that, as the reader knows, was a time when gods, not men, reigned in Egypt.

***

By the mid-1980s the use of advanced technology as an archaeological tool arrived in Egypt. French teams, then Japanese, began to probe the Giza monuments with soil-penetrating radar and other high-tech equipment. They discovered puzzling "cavities" all over the place—and gave rise to a new set of mysteries.

In May 1986 a team of two French architects, Gilles Dormion and Jean-Patrice Goidin, were somehow allowed to go into the Great Pyramid with instruments identified as a "gravity meter" and they *"discovered previously unknown spaces behind walls eight feet thick in the corridor leading to the so-called Queen's Chamber,"* to quote one of the many press reports; this one, from the *Economist* of London, contained almost in passing a revelation whose significance loomed larger later on: The high-tech equipment was that used by engineers to detect dangerous structural cracks in *nuclear plants*.

The focus of their findings was the **Horizontal Passage** that leads to the **"Queen's Chamber"** from a junction where the Ascending Passage becomes the Grand Gallery (fig. 24). The nature and extent of the voids or "spaces" found behind the western wall of this horizontal passage was unclear, but speculation quickly arose that the suspected cavity was a long-sought royal "Treasure Chamber."

In September 1986 the two Frenchmen, now openly on a mission on behalf of the French national energy company Electricité de France, returned to the pyramid—accompanied by geophysical experts of EdF who took charge of the operation. When the gravity-testing equipment reconfirmed the existence of *an elongated "cavity" behind the corridor's western wall,* they used high-speed power tools to drill three holes through the wall toward the mysterious cavity; the idea, it was explained at the time, was to insert an endoscopic camera to find out what the cavity might hold.

To their amazement, after drilling through some six feet of hard stone, the drilling equipment hit a two-foot layer of "Royal Limestone"—a rare limestone that was used in antiquity only for sculptures, being too soft for structural use. *And then the drills reached a layer of*

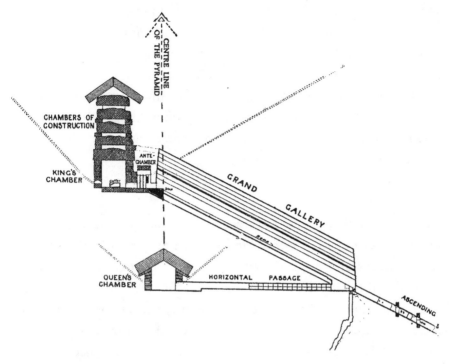

Figure 24

sand. It was a very unusual kind of sand, according to what was published—a "powdery fine sand," totally different from the sand of the Giza plateau.

What was one to make of all that? Both the highest Egyptian authorities—and the head of the scientific section in the French Ministry of Foreign Affairs—were summoned. The published reports on the discovery (which occurred on September 6, 1986) stated that Dr. Ahmed Kadry, the new Chairman of the Egyptian Antiquities Organization, who personally collected samples of the unusual sand into a plastic bag, described the sand as "more precious than gold." The French representatives took samples of the sand for laboratory tests in France.

Two days later, on September 8th, the Egyptian authorities ordered all the work stopped, and everyone was told to go home.

While there was never an official announcement regarding the tests' results, subsequent information circulated in Cairo that the sand "was apparently imported from another part of Egypt, was subsequently sifted, and then *enriched with minerals* before being placed in the pyramid by the ancient architects" (*Reuters* news agency March 6, 1987, report by its Cairo correspondent; emphasis mine).

To use a metaphor, the amazing find of the mysterious sand disappeared under the sands of time; except that it triggered a chain of events that resulted in the discovery of a secret chamber—by me and two teammates, as I will soon tell.

***

After the French, Japanese researchers from Tokyo's Waseda University arrived in Giza with another kind of high-tech equipment (an electromagnetic scanner rather than the French microgravimetric instruments). By directing electromagnetic waves into the soil at an angle, they could determine what lay buried—a structure, artifacts, or a cavity. They received permission to examine the Sphinx and its surroundings, but in time they also re-checked the spot in the passage to the Queen's Chamber where the French had drilled.

The Japanese team spent in Giza ten days in January–February 1987. Their findings drew renewed attention to the enigma of the Sphinx. Newspapers were filled with "Sphinx news" (see examples from the *Christian Science Monitor* of Boston, the *Daily Yomiuri* of Tokyo, and *Pravda* in Moscow, fig. 25). They reported the discovery of several underground cavities at or near the Sphinx—and especially one that suggested the existence of a tunnel linking the Sphinx and the Great Pyramid.

Their request for permission to explore the tunnel possibility by going down inside the pyramid to what is called the Pit, was denied. Indeed, the existence of the varied "cavities" and "tunnel" made the Egyptian authorities uneasy and reluctant to allow any further exploration at all. The chairman of the Egyptian Antiquities Organization, Dr. Ahmed Kadry, was prominently reported to have stated that he would call a worldwide symposium of Egyptologists to evaluate all these new finds before more work would be allowed.

Saturday, January 31, 1987

THE DAILY YOMIURI

Underground Spaces Found Near Sphinx

By Kikuro Takagi
Yomiuri Shimbun Correspondent

CAIRO—An excavation team from Tokyo's Waseda University succeeded in discovering underground caverns in the area around the Sphinx at the foot of the Giza Plateau Thursday.

The team used a newly-developed machine capable of detecting objects by echolocation. A simil...

Cheops.

The team also found a chamber in the ground in front of the Sphinx, and more secrets of ancient Egypt are expected to be discovered.

Last year, a French team made two attempts to bore small holes in the wall near the queen's chamber, but had to stop the search because of technical probl...

SCIENCE BRIEFS
ARCHAEOLOGY

Great Pyramid may have undiscovered chambers

Undiscovered chambers in the 5,000-year-old Great Pyramid at Giza, Egypt, may contain treasures, say Japanese scientists who are exploring the building.

This vast ... e, built with ... araoh Cheops ... a thousand ... hamen, is a ... ystery, says ... a of Waseda

... probing its ... romagnetic ... found the ... a passage ... d Queen's ... vhich they ... ted for 90 ... ide of the ... lieved to ... of granite ... hat the ... ded the ... ut as a ... of the ... m the ... est the

SCIENCE AND TECHNOLOGY ABROAD

Tunnel to the Sphinx

2/9/87

CAIRO, 8. (Pravda staff corr.) Japanese scientists from Waseda University in Tokyo who have been studying the Cheops Pyramid have made an important discovery. With the help of the latest equipment, which uses electromagnetic waves to penetrate through the stone mass of the pyramid, they discovered a previously unknown chamber and a tunnel leading toward the sphynx. On the whole, the research confirmed the conjecture that 10 to 15 percent of the pyramid's

volume is comprised of empty spaces, the exact location, and purpose of which are not yet clear.

Final results on the size and possible content of the areas discovered by the Japanese will become known in the middle of April, when computer processing of the data will be completed. However, many scientists already believe that modern methods of pyramid research herald a revolution in Egyptology.

V. BELYAKOV.

... news Services

Post-Intelligencer, Seattle

... of experts in archaeology, includ-

Figure 25

The scientific conclave was never called. But the interest in the Sphinx, revived by the Japanese researchers, led to other developments that had an impact on the main issue—the age of the Giza Pyramids: New ways emerged for dating all the Giza monuments by dating just one of them, the Sphinx.

Now, to determine the age of the Sphinx—the *original* Sphinx—is no simple task. Drawings from Napoleon's visit to Egypt showed the Sphinx buried in sands up to its neck; visitors stood on sands that high even in the nineteenth century (fig. 26). In fact, once excavations carried

Figure 26

out in the 1920s uncovered the full body of the Sphinx, a stela was discovered between its paws in which the Pharaoh Thothmes IV recorded how he dug the Sphinx out of the sand dunes that covered it up to its neck—already in 1400 B.C.!

As anyone who had visited Giza in contemporary times *(and before it was "restored" by being completely covered with fresh masonry in the 1990s)* could easily see, the exposed Sphinx displayed two different body parts. Though carved out of natural bedrock, the lower parts and paws of the Sphinx were covered or "fleshed out" with masonry (fig. 27). It is known that such repairs or restorations with masonry had already taken place in 1400 B.C., in 700 B.C., and in the first and second centuries A.D.; some historians believe that similar restoration had even taken place in the time of Chefra, the presumed builder of the Sphinx. So these lower parts cannot serve to determine the original age of the Sphinx.

The upper parts—the main body and the head—retained their natural bedrock origin; and those upper parts reveal severe erosion, running

Figure 27

along horizontal strata (fig. 28). It has been generally assumed that this erosion was caused over time by the desert winds; but in the mid 1980s the author-researcher John Anthony West, in his book *Serpent in the Sky* and varied articles, suggested that the "weathering" on the Sphinx was due to erosion by *water,* not wind and windblown sand; and known ancient climate conditions and dates of wetter periods *"made the Sphinx older than 10,000 B.C."*

This novel approach found, in 1990, support from an unexpected quarter in the person of Dr. Robert M. Schoch, a respected geologist at Boston University. In 1991 he was joined by Dr. Thomas Dobecki, a Houston-based geophysicist, in a presentation to the Geological Society of America in which they reported that their on-site researches confirmed the *weathering by water,* resulting in *dating the Sphinx "to 7000 B.C. or earlier."*

As with other challenges to established Egyptological tenets, that too—after more presentations, articles, TV programs, debates, and debunkings—ended up being ignored by the Egyptological establishment.

Figure 28

***

By 1990, Egypt witnessed a wave of a new breed of tourists—"New Agers" attracted by the stream of findings dating the Giza pyramids and Sphinx to much earlier times. Arriving by the hundreds and thousands, they came to see the handiwork of Extraterrestrials, Atlantis survivors, Osirians, or whomever—and to hear in lectures, conferences, and conventions what all that portends for the future.

In 1992 I was again in Egypt, as a presenter at one such conference. The venue was the exclusive Mena House, a palatial hotel first built in the1890s to accommodate royalty. It is situated literally at the foot of the Giza promontory on which the pyramids and Sphinx stand, and it is a unique thrill to dine in the hotel's grand restaurant with the Great Pyramid looming over you through the large windows.

The hotel's lounge, with its bar, tables, sofas, and corner recesses was where the "action" was after the formal lectures and meetings. It took no time to discover that the place was abuzz with rumors of what had "really been found" in secret chambers, what is hidden, why access is blocked here and there. It also took no time for two men to invite me to join them there for a drink. Among the varied messages that the hotel's staff slipped to guests under the rooms' doors, I found in mine an envelope with two business cards: One was of Dr. Alexander Shumilin, Chief of the Middle East Bureau of *Pravda;* the other, of Dmitri Veliki, Middle East Correspondent of *Izvestia.* They represented, respectively, the official dailies of the Soviet Government and the Soviet Communist Party; they were, as one had to unquestionably assume, agents of the KGB (the Soviet spy organization). I was too curious not to accept the invitation.

They spoke good English and were obviously well informed in all matters of the Near East—politics, economics, history, and current affairs. They were also well informed about me, and about my books, including *The Wars of Gods and Men* that followed the first two. In *The 12th Planet* I dealt with the Sumerian Anunnaki gods and their coming to Earth from the planet Nibiru; in *The Stairway to Heaven* I dealt with the post-Diluvial spaceport in the Sinai peninsula and the construction of the Giza complex as part of the space facilities; and in the third book I dealt with the wars among the Anunnaki clans, including the "Pyramid Wars," and the destruction of the spaceport with nuclear weapons.

It was the latter that interested the two Russians most. As they and I measured our words, the reason for the meeting began to emerge from their line of questions. What could I tell them beyond what is in the books? Do the Sumerian texts describe the weapons used in the Pyramid Wars? Would I name the mountain which in my opinion is the true Mount Sinai? Where precisely was the wiped out spaceport? Do the Sumerian texts provide a clue regarding what kind of nuclear explosion it was? Did I know that the mysterious sand found by the French was from the Sinai peninsula? Did I hear the rumors that the sand was radioactive?

They (I hoped) learned little from my evasive answers (the Cold War with the Soviet Union was still raging); I thought that I had learned a lot from them: ***Something significant, some important secret, had to do with the enigmatic sand discovered in the "Queen's Chamber" passage; and the Soviets saw a nuclear connection to the Anunnaki spaceport in the Sinai.***

These were implications that had to be pursued.

When the lecture sessions of the conference for which I came were over, the participants embarked on their tour & sightseeing program; I decided to stay behind and rejoin the group only for the flight back. My first undertaking was to visit the ARCE office-cum-library in Cairo. It had been six years since the French had found the sand, and I was curious what had transpired since then.

Yes, I was told, there have been reports about the sand, but no direct information regarding the results of the tests conducted in France; it was Egyptian tests of the sand samples that they retained that showed it was similar in its makeup to sand found in the Sinai, in the area of el-Tor (an ancient port on the Red Sea that served Egyptian mining of turquoise in the Sinai). Why would the Pyramid's builders haul sand from a hundred miles away when sand is plentiful right there in Giza? My guess, they said, was as good as anyone's. They gave me the address of the EdF in Paris to whom I could write (I later did, but never received a straight answer).

Is it true, I asked, that sections of the Pyramid—like the Queen's Chamber—have been off limits? Yes, now and then. They tipped me off that the best time to poke around inside the Great Pyramid was right after the official closing time, when the Pyramid's guards keep it open for about an hour to accommodate visitors who stay to meditate after the crowds are gone.

The ARCE library had a copy of a book-report written by the two French architects; it dealt with the architectural aspects of the Great Pyramid, but had nothing about the sand tests. I also found in the library a detailed report written (in English, in 1987) by Prof. Sakuji Yoshimura and three other professors of Waseda University about the Giza findings of the Japanese researchers. Part 6 dealt with their "Non-destructive Pyramid Investigation by Electromagnetic Wave Method." I was especially interested in the pages dealing with the Queen's Chamber, and the ARCE librarian allowed me to make photostatic copies.

The Japanese reported that the existence of an elongated cavity *in the Horizontal Passage* to the Queen's Chamber "has been confirmed, as well as the presence, in the cavity, *of quantities of sand,* in agreement with the French microgravimetric measurements" (emphasis mine). The report disclosed that there was also indication of a hidden cavity in the Queen's Chamber itself in the **western wall**—but its extent could not be defined due to unexplained "turbulent reflections" that disturbed the readings.

***

Those revelations were in line with beliefs held by various previous explorers that the builders of the Great Pyramid offset its immense weight by strategically placed gabled arches and cavities. The Japanese, who suspected a cavity behind the *western* wall of the Queen's Chamber, noted in their report that the **eastern** wall of that chamber, where the ceiling was gabled, contains "a niche which was symbolically corbeled."

The reference was to a well-known feature in the Queen's Chamber known as **The Niche** (as shown schematically in fig. 29). It is usually considered to have been a wall recess for holding a statue, of a god or of a king. Past visitors to the chamber could see damage to the Niche's stone masonry caused by varied burrowing efforts (starting, it is believed, with Al Mamoon's men) to find out what might lie behind it (fig. 30). The opening has been known to extend inward, as a tunnel, a short distance (the 1971 comprehensive study *Secrets of the Great Pyramid* by Peter Tompkins states that "treasure seekers have hacked a passage through the back [of the Niche] for several yards").

The Niche and its opening, cleaned of debris (plate 3), were the obvious feature of the Queen's Chamber when I visited it on previous occasions (in addition, prominent are the openings of "air shafts" in the north and south walls). Now again in Cairo, I wondered why the Niche did not arouse the curiosity of the French or the Japanese: Neither of them made any mention of exploring *in the eastern wall;* and that was odd.

Figure 29

Figure 30

The next day I entered the Great Pyramid in time for the extra "quiet hour." I made my way up the Ascending Passage. At the junction to the Horizontal Passage there was a gate of metal bars that was not there on previous visits—but it was open (fig. 31). Advancing half-crouching through the low and narrow Horizontal Passage that leads to the Queen's Chamber (for most of its length, it is less than 4 x 4 feet high and wide) I looked for the three holes bored in the western wall by the French, but couldn't find them. I reached the lighted Queen's Chamber,

Figure 31

where it is possible to stand up. There was no one there—but someone was watching: *I noticed surveillance video cameras* at two corners of the ceiling; one was pointed toward the entrance to the Chamber, the other to the Niche in the eastern wall. *And the hole in the Niche was now covered by a wire mesh in a wooden frame* (plate 4).

There was something else new there: SAND. On the exposed ledge of stone masonry in front of the covered opening there was a small pile of sand. It looked like ordinary sand, but it was an unusual sand: mixed into it were blue-green granules. A mineral? Plastic? I could not tell. The words in the Reuters 1987 report about the unusual sand discovered by the French having been "mixed with minerals" flashed back in my memory; so did the Russians' queries about radioactive sand.

Was that what I was seeing? Where did it come from? There was no sand on the floor or anywhere else. I managed to remove the covering in its wooden frame, and shined my flashlight into the squarish opening; I saw a dark tunnel-like space. Did the sand come from inside there? I couldn't tell.

What was I to do? It was eerie enough to be alone in the belly of the pyramid, engulfed by complete silence but watched by unknown eyes. I was seized with a fear that someone, routinely or on purpose, would shut the metal barrier at the passage's entrance and lock me in, at least for the night if not for longer. I had in my jacket's pocket several of the hotel's message envelopes, so I used one to shovel some of the peculiar sand into another, and took it with me. I believe I remembered to put the covering back. Cold-sweating, I reached the gate at the passage's entrance; it was open. I rushed up and out—relieved, but bewildered: Who was digging behind the Niche, and what lay there, deeper inside?

Back in New York I tested the sand with a regular radiation reader; there was no unusual radiation level. The Department of Geology at the University of Cincinnati analyzed the sand, at my request, in May 1993, finding its quartz grains unusually coated with iron oxide; the "blue minute flakes" appeared to be shavings of "an artificial or man-made material" (e.g., plastic); there was no mention of radioactivity.

So the Queen's Chamber mystery remained: Where did the sand come from? Why was it mixed with the peculiar granules? Was it the same sand "mixed with minerals" as was reported in the French borings? Why was it all kept a secret?

It was a new puzzle. Yet, when a few years later an opportunity arose to find answers, an even greater mystery was encountered.

3

THE SECRET CHAMBER

I f you look up the word *Destiny* in the dictionary, you will find it explained as Fate; if you look up *Fate,* you will read that it means Destiny. But the ancient Sumerians made a great distinction between the two: Destiny, NAM, was not only predetermined, it was also final and unavoidable—as human mortality, for example. Fate was change-able, was subject to free choice: By being just, by following moral com-mandments, for example, one could live longer; Fate was NAM.TAR, a destiny that could be "twisted" and postponed (though not avoided).

I have pondered more than once which one it was—Fate or Destiny—that, unrealized by me, started in 1992 a chain of unfore-seen events that led, step by step, to a major discovery and almost to my death.

The international conference at which I lectured in 1992 was arranged by an outfit called Power Places Tours. As I later learned, a competitor of theirs, a Mr. Abbas Nadim, sneaked into the conference hall and took note of the speakers. Contacting me back in the USA, he introduced himself as an Egyptian tour operator with an office in Los Angeles. He invited me to be a "Tour Scholar" on tours organized by his company, Visions Travel & Tours.

I told him that what I really wanted was to have my own tours, leading my own fans to sites of my choice. No problem, he said; I have the best contacts in Egypt; where do you want to go? I told him that I wanted to go to the Sinai, in search of the true Mount Sinai—for which I'd need a helicopter. I did not expect to hear from him again, for everyone told me that with the Sinai (returned to the Egyptians by Israel in a peace treaty) still a military zone, private helicopter flights were out of the question. To my surprise, he called after a while to say it could be done. The result was an April 1994 Egypt & Sinai "In the Footsteps of the Exodus" Tour—the first tour group allowed by the Egyptians into the Sinai, and to do so through a previously military tunnel under the Suez Canal.

Abbas—everyone called him just by his first name—did obtain for me a helicopter, but the planned landing with it on the Mount could not take place (those and subsequent adventures connected with Mount Sinai are described in *The Earth Chronicles Expeditions*). In Egypt proper, he arranged for us to see archaeological sites indicated by me that were usually excluded from tourist itineraries. But we could not enter the Queen's Chamber; it was out of bounds due to the *"Gantenbrink Affair"*: The previous year a German engineer, Rudolph Gantenbrink, who was hired by the Egyptians to install a ventilating/dehumidifying system in the Great Pyramid, brought in a tiny robotic rover equipped with headlights and a camera and sent it up a shaft in the Queen's Chamber's southern wall (seen in plate 3; another one of two misnamed "air shafts" is in the opposite northern wall). The very narrow shaft is channel-like, about eight inches square. On the way up the robot found that the channel was blocked by a stone plug. The discovery made worldwide headlines; it also infuriated the Egyptian authorities, who accused Gantenbrink of unauthorized explorations and premature disclosures. The result was a ban on entry to the Queen's Chamber . . .

We tried nevertheless, but the metal door leading to the horizontal passage was indeed locked. We'll go in next time, Abbas assured me—and we did.

***

The next time was a "Peace Tour" in February 1995—Egypt, Sinai, Jordan, and Israel—an itinerary made possible by the signing of a peace treaty between Israel and Jordan. In the Sinai, Abbas had to obtain for me another helicopter; in Egypt, the visit had to include entry into the Queen's Chamber. He achieved both.

How he had obtained the helicopter, I was not supposed to ask. The admission to the Queen's Chamber was attained with the help of the new Chief of the Giza Plateau Antiquities—none other than my early recommender **Dr. Zahi Hawass,** with whom Abbas had become personally friendly.

At the time admission to the Great Pyramid was allowed "By permit only," and the Sphinx was completely out of bounds, due to a Restoration Project (overseen by Dr. Hawass) that required extensive scaffolding while the Sphinx was being covered with new masonry from head to tail. Many have suspected that the Sphinx Restoration Project was really a cover-up—figuratively and literally, a way to put an end to the mushrooming speculation about the age of the Sphinx and the suspected "cavities" in and around it.

But not only was our group allowed to enter the Sphinx enclosure, stand between its paws, and explore around it—Dr. Hawass himself came to welcome us (fig. 32), and let me peek into a just-discovered chamberlike "cavity" in the back of the Sphinx (fig. 33, with my wife). It was a gracious gesture for which I later sent him a letter of thanks, enclosing press clippings showing him escorting America's First Lady and her daughter at these Sphinx discoveries.

From the Sphinx we walked to the Great Pyramid; we were the last group to be let in. Once inside the Queen's Chamber, I was astounded by changes to the Niche's hollowed-out opening and to its covering—as this photo (plate 5), when compared to previous ones, shows. It was obvious that someone was conducting some work there. Was it part of the previous year's ventilating efforts, or did someone continue to tunnel deeper inside?

I asked Abbas to send the group back to our hotel, but stay with me for a while longer. I also asked one of the group, John Cogswell, a

Figure 32

Figure 33

veteran of the first journey, to stay behind. Once all others had left, I told the two of them the story of the sand, and of the visible changes in the Niche. "I would like to find out what's inside, where the tunneling leads to," I said; "because if the sand came from inside, there could be a 'cavity' there—a secret chamber."

The challenge was irresistible. We removed the framed wire covering, shined our flashlights in, strained to see what's inside; we couldn't see much beyond several feet; but what we could see was astounding: *Lengths of plastic pipes were strewn about* (plate 6) *and even a discarded bottle; someone had been doing some unreported work inside!*

John Cogswell, an attorney, a graduate of Yale University in history, and a former U.S. Marines officer, volunteered to climb in. Crawling with flashlight and camera, he shouted at intervals to let us know he was OK. Then we could barely hear him. For a while Abbas and I began to wonder whether something went wrong. Then we heard Cogswell again, and saw the light of his flashlight moving toward us (plate 7).

When he re-emerged at long last (plate 8), catching his breath he shouted to us: **"There's a secret chamber in there!"**

Excitedly, he told us what he had found. I sketched on a cover of my Briefing Notes what he was describing (fig. 34); he later sent me a professional sketch showing him inside the secret chamber (fig. 35). But the best way to tell the whole story is to quote his own words in a sworn affidavit that he prepared as a historic record:

AFFIDAVIT OF JOHN M. COGSWELL

In early February 1995 I was on a Visions Travel tour featuring Zecharia Sitchin. Our first stop was to see the Giza pyramids near Cairo, Egypt. There was hardly anyone at the pyramids when we arrived. As I recall, we were the only bus and there were a few vendors around peddling their wares. We entered the pyramid and looked around. Part of our visit included the Queen's Chamber.

When we entered the Queen's Chamber, we noticed a hole in the lower part of the niche, on the left as one enters. After everyone left

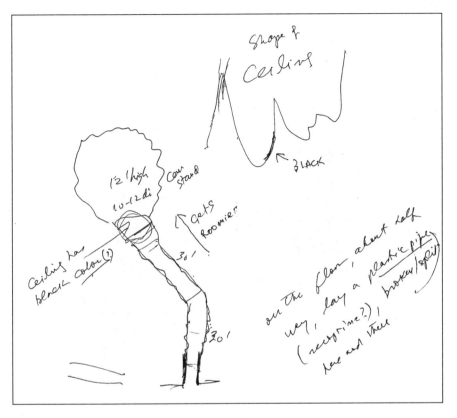

Figure 34

except Zecharia Sitchin, Abbas Nadim and myself, I removed a few boards in the area of the niche to clear the entry way. I then took a flashlight and crawled in the hole. I crawled along for about 15 feet when a tunnel veered to the left. Along this way, I noted some old black plastic pipe that was badly damaged. The tunnel during this first stage of the journey was approximately 2.5 feet square. I took photos. After the first 15 feet, the tunnel veered to the left approximately 30–45° and continued for about another 15 feet. As I went on, the tunnel got roomier. At the end, I entered into an area roughly circular in nature and approximately 10–12 feet in diameter from the waist up and approximately 12 feet high. It was not a finished room but appeared to be a room created by the removal of building stones. I saw the building stones which were not removed on my left as I stood up.

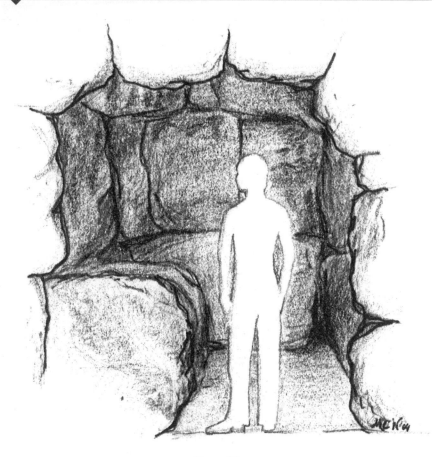

Figure 35

These stones were as high as my waist and made the diameter below my waist approximately 6–8 feet in diameter. The stones were unfinished. The ceiling of the room was uneven.

I am told by Zecharia Sitchin, who was present at the time, that I reported seeing black on the upper ceiling stones in one area, though today I no longer recall having made this statement. I recall drawing a sketch of what I had witnessed on a paper of Zecharia Sitchin. He subsequently xeroxed the paper and added certain language. A copy of this paper is attached.

There were present with me during this adventure Zecharia Sitchin and Abbas Nadim. No one else was present. I took photographs and have attached them to this affidavit with a legend pertaining to the view of each of them. In order to give one a sense of what I experienced, I have asked a local artist, Michelle Wayland, to do an artistic rendering from the pictures, Zecharia Sitchin's paper, this affidavit and my memory. A copy of this is also attached.

Signed this 28th day of January 2004.

Cogswell accompanied the affidavit with several photographs. The first one reproduced here (plate 9) represents a look backward to the entryway after crawling in, showing lengths of plastic pipes and a ribbed plastic (?) container lying on the tunnel's floor. The second one (plate 10) is near the entrance to the secret chamber (note the blackened lintel stone). Next (plate 11) is looking into the chamber. Plate 12 shows the chamber's upper part and its (blackened) ceiling. The next photograph (plate 13) shows the chamber's walls and some of its ceiling stones. Plate 14, taken on the way back, shows the tunnel's stonework toward the exit.

The Cogswell photographs and his verbal description suggest that the chamber and the tunnel to it had been excavated in earlier times; they might have even been part of the original construction. His description divides the tunnel into two different segments. The first is narrow and runs straight from the opening in the Niche for about 15 feet; the continuation veers there to the left and is roomier. This second section runs for about another 15 feet, reaching the chamber. Does this mean that the two segments were dug at different times, or that the original builders attempted concealment? Did the builders, as in other known instances (like the barrier found in the shaft by the Gantenbrink robot), intentionally put up a barrier or two—at 15 feet where the tunnel veers left, and by erecting the wall of the Niche itself? Did they insert a layer of sand behind the barrier(s), as the French have found in the cavity in the Horizontal Passage leading to the Queen's Chamber?

But no matter what had happened in earlier times, what about the recent mystery of the Niche coverings, surveillance cameras, and the puzzling SAND that I have found?

In addition to the initial photo taken from the Queen's Chamber and showing red and black plastic pipes (plate 6), Cogswell's photos also show, in the first 15 feet into the tunnel, **discarded plastic piping.** *This is most incriminating in regard to the present mystery: It indicates that diggers were in the tunnel* in recent times. *Were they the same ones* who also installed the surveillance cameras and covered the Niche's hollow?

Did they enter farther in, reach a barrier, then break through it and find sand, as the French did in the passage? And, most importantly, *did they stop there, without continuing to find the chamber?* That was highly unlikely: Once the sand behind the barrier was removed (Cogswell did not see any sand), *they must have gone on and discovered the chamber back inside. So WHO were they, and WHY was it kept a secret?*

At my request, the three of us agreed to say nothing about the discovery, to see WHO will some day disclose the existence of the unknown chamber—and thereby confess to the secret digging and reveal WHAT might have been found there. **But, as far as I know, so far no one did.**

The authoritative *The Complete Pyramids* states this in regard to the Queen's Chamber and the Niche (of which it shows a photo):

> The so-called Queen's Chamber was certainly not for the burial of a queen. Very probably it was a sealed room for a special statue of the king, representing his *Ka* or "spiritual force." This is suggested by the existence of a corbeled niche, 4.7 m (15 ft. 5 in. high, on the east wall of the chamber, which may once have held such a statue. A square pit at its base was deepened by early treasure seekers.

The book, dated **1997,** thus *makes no mention of a chamber deeper inside.* The book's author, Dr. Mark Lehner, has collaborated with Dr. Hawass in numerous Giza projects; what he says can be taken to be the official word of the Egyptian Antiquities Authority. Articles in the press and Internet sites continue, to this date—ten years later—to state that the tunnel is "a ***blind*** passageway."

So this chapter is the first time that the existence of this secret chamber, and how and with whom I had discovered it, is publicly disclosed.

4

THE FATEFUL DAY

A fter the 1995 visit to Egypt that culminated with the discovery of the secret chamber, one more thing remained on my list of "must see" there: To enter the Relieving Chambers and examine the red paint markings—the sole "evidence" supporting the Khufu-built-it "Holy Grail" of Egyptologists, and the one I had suggested was a forgery.

I broached the subject to Abbas, urging him to use his good standing with Dr. Hawass (whose new titles, including Secretary General, Supreme Council of Antiquities, reflected his increasing authority). Abbas promised to "work on it." But the time for another group tour of Egypt was not right: Tourists began to be targets of murderous terrorist attacks; and the attacks included the shooting up of tour buses—even at the entrance to the Egyptian Museum in Cairo!—that belonged to the transportation company Abbas was using . . . We changed destinations, and arranged several tours to sites in the Americas of which I have also been writing.

Egyptian antiquities were also beset by other problems, besides terrorism. The "Gantenbrink Affair" left a lingering bitterness; the European press, in particular, felt that Gantenbrink was mistreated, and it questioned why has there been no follow-up to the discovery of the barrier (in the southern "air shaft"). The delay gave rise to speculation and conspiracy suspicions. Why is discovery avoided? What is being hidden?

In the United States, the West-Schoch claims continued to sizzle, especially after the admitted "Sphinx cavities" discoveries. Was there indeed a "Hall of Records" under the Sphinx as Edgar Cayce had predicted? Reviving its Giza involvements, the A.R.E. sponsored (in 1996) a new high-tech research project, led by Dr. Joseph Schor of New York. It came to an abrupt halt due to frenzied media publicity that included a TV documentary, "The Mystery of the Sphinx," which angered the Egyptian authorities. It all fueled a climate of distrust and speculation.

As the Sphinx Conservation Program—a favorite of Dr. Hawass—progressed and the familiar ancient monument began to disappear under fresh masonry (fig. 36), the "true" motives for the project came into questioning. Archaeological and related journals were filled with accusations, explanations, and rebuttals. The atmosphere of suspicions and recriminations was reinforced by reports that "outsiders" have been selectively allowed up into the Relieving Chambers. In spite of constant claims by the authorities that the Relieving Chambers were inaccessible, photographs began to appear in Europe of (unidentified) visitors up there (figs. 37, 38). The photographs revealed extensive graffiti all over the place, *some with dates going back to 1839 (Vyse's time!),* much of it with 1940s dates—identifiable as the handiwork of British military personnel who swarmed inside the pyramids during World War II—but some possibly much more recent. The photographs also captured inscribed cartouches (fig. 39). Visitors to the Great pyramid began to report that some kind of work was being carried on above the King's Chamber.

In view of all that, I pressed Abbas to use his contacts with Hawass to let me in too. Abbas and I were planning at the time a tour of Israel, and I felt that it was now-or-never for my chance to see the "quarry marks" (as Howard Vyse had called them). The tour—"A Unique Expedition to the Holy Land with Zecharia Sitchin"—was finally set for September 1997 (fig. 40), but adding an "Egypt extension" to the group's eleven days in Israel was impractical. I therefore suggested to Abbas that just he

Figure 36

and I should go to Egypt from Israel after the group tour ended—if he could get his friend Hawass to let us in.

As the tour date was nearing, Abbas came through. Calling from Los Angeles, "I obtained the permission from Zahi [Hawass]," he triumphantly told me.

Seventeen years after writing about the Great Pyramid Forgery in *The Stairway to Heaven,* I was finally going to enter the "scene of the crime."

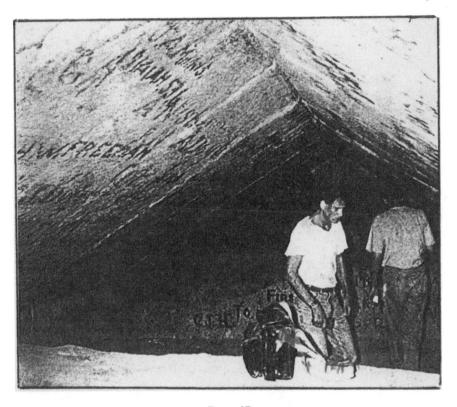

Figure 37

Figure 38

Figure 39

***

Among my fans who registered for the Israel tour was Wallace M. Wally, as all who knew him called him—a recognized authority on prosthetics and other technical wizardry and a veteran of previous tours whose ability to take pictures even in restricted circumstances made him my "tour photographer." He was the right person to take along to witness and record what we would find up there, in the narrow chambers; and I spoke to him about it. He readily agreed to join me on the side trip to Egypt—a detour that required a different flight plan, with Lufthansa via Frankfurt.

Abbas added Wally's name to the list pre-submitted to the office of the Director of Giza Antiquities, describing him as my photographer; in fact I had an additional confidential task for Wally, for which he took along some of his small tools: To try to get a sample of the red ink with which the "quarry marks" were inscribed, to be analyzed for their age. I felt that this was important, not only because of my forgery conclusions, but also having in mind the Perry remark quoted in the first chapter: That the red paint used for the inscriptions "was a composition of red ochre called by the Arabs 'moghrah' which is still in use"—*"still in use"* in his time—a remark whose implications for archaeological forg-

VISIONS TRAVEL
& TOURS, INC.

IS PROUD TO ANNOUNCE A UNIQUE EXPEDITION

TO THE

HOLY LAND

WITH

ZECHARIA SITCHIN

SEPTEMBER 14-25, 1997

WAS JERUSALEM A "MISSION CONTROL CENTER" OF EXTRATERRESTRIALS?

''THE HIDDEN EVIDENCE''

On this unique Expedition, the best-selling author of The Earth Chronicles, Genesis Revisited, and Divine Encounters will lead a select, limited group on the most comprehensive tour of Jerusalem's Holy Shrines, underground excavations, and unmatched museums to see the oldest foundations of the Temple Mount, the Rock of Ark of the Covenant, The Qabbalah Center of Safed, and archaeological evidence spanning six millenia -- as well as a tour of Mediterranean resorts, Mt. Carmel, the Sea of Galilee, Nazareth, Bethlehem, the Dead Sea, the Caves of Qumran, and Massada.

LIMITED PARTICIPATION

Figure 40

ery made one wonder whether the paint's use has continued beyond the nineteenth century A.D. . . . .

And so it was that on September 25th, 1997, after the group left Israel early in the morning on the flight back to the USA, the three of us—Abbas, Wally, and me—left in the evening on a flight to Cairo. We were met there by Abass's Cairo office manager, who drove us to our hotel—the Mena House, right next to the pyramids.

It was a short and mostly sleepless night; yet I was, as I recall, the very first hotel guest to come to the restaurant for breakfast in the morning, choosing a seat for a full view of the Great Pyramid. It loomed large, overwhelming, and beckoning—as if challenging me with its secrets, as if saying: *Try, if you can . . .*

When Abbas and Wally joined me, I outlined to them a plan of action. I had with me the sketches, copied from Vyse's book, of the red-ink markings and their location, and prepared a sheet with the cartouche-containing ones, fig. 41 (oddly, all the cartouches appeared to be upside down, as though painted by someone lying on his back). Since I had no idea of how we would enter the chambers or for how long, I

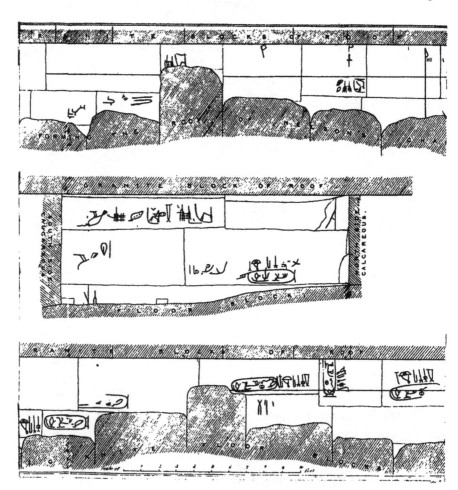

Figure 41

made three sets, one for each one of us. Then, loaded with cameras with both black & white and color films, flashlights, sheets, pens, and excited anticipation, we were driven by Abbas's local manager up the road to the pyramids.

We first had to make a stop at the nearby administration office, where—so Abbas had arranged with Hawass—one of Hawass's deputies was to take us into the Great Pyramid and up to the Relieving Chambers; an array of ladders was supposed to be ready there for us. While I and Wally remained in the car, Abbas went in to get the deputy director. We expected the procedure to take just a few minutes, but Abbas did not return after ten minutes, and after twenty minutes; half an hour passed—and Abbas was still in there . . .

I decided to go in and see what was causing the delay. Wally, loaded with his cameras, came with me. We were told that Abbas was "inside," meeting with Dr. Hawass. We were allowed into the Director's office, and Hawass greeted me and invited me to sit down beside his desk, next to Abbas. I looked at Abbas, and he just raised an eyebrow, giving me no clue as to what was causing the delay.

Abbas was discussing with me his plan for a conference on board an Alaska cruise ship, Hawass said to me; what do you (meaning I) think? Well, anything Abbas undertakes is worthwhile, I answered. Hawass then shifted the conversation to other subjects—none relating to the purpose of our being there that morning. I wondered what was going on.

As the aimless conversation continued, it became obvious that Hawass was just killing time. Then it became clear why: His deputy— the one who was supposed to take us into the Great Pyramid—showed up with a newspaper which he had obtained in town. It was a daily newspaper known for its nationalistic positions, and it had a long article that criticized the government for allowing foreigners to "defile Egypt's heritage" under the guise of archaeology. A segment was devoted to the foreigners who promote the idea that the Great Pyramid and Sphinx were built by Atlanteans or by extraterrestrials, thereby implying that the Egyptians themselves were incapable of such achievements. It was an insult to Egypt's national pride, the article stated.

So that was what Hawass was discussing with Abbas, waiting for the newspaper to be brought from the city! After the relevant paragraphs were read and translated, Hawass said to me: You will understand that in view of this attack I cannot let you go in, take pictures, and proclaim again that Khufu did not build the Pyramid . . .

I was shocked. This is bad—this is ominous, I thought; perhaps one should have seen it coming—the terrorist attacks on foreign tourists, the abrupt stopping of certain exploration projects. But I could not accept such an abrupt stop to *my* project . . . Overcoming my shock, I vehemently protested: The three of us came to Egypt just for that, based on an explicit promise from you to let us in, I told Hawass; How can you go back on your word?

Speaking to his deputy and to Abbas in Arabic, Hawass finally asked me and Wally to wait outside. A short while later Abbas came out. Hawass is very embarrassed, he said; so he will let you in—***but no pictures;*** we must leave the cameras behind—there must not be any photographic record of this visit. I tried to protest, but Abbas said that Hawass overruled his deputy for this compromise: Go in without cameras, or not at all. I gave Wally an inquisitive look, and he responded with a slight nod. So be it, I told Abbas. We went out to the car, and the Egyptian aide, riding with us to the Pyramid, collected all the cameras and locked them in the car's trunk.

***

We entered the Pyramid through the familiar entrance, going all the way up through the majestic Grand Gallery (fig. 42). Where it ends, a large flat stone block known as the "Great Step" forms a platform in front of the ante-chamber that leads to the King's Chamber (fig. 43). Reaching it and stopping there, we saw that above us workmen were standing on a ledge; from there, we assumed, the way would lead farther up to the Crawlway leading to Davison's Chamber, and then via Vyse's vertical Forced Passage enter the upper Relieving Chambers (see fig. 17, page 24). Hawass's deputy shouted to them and they lowered

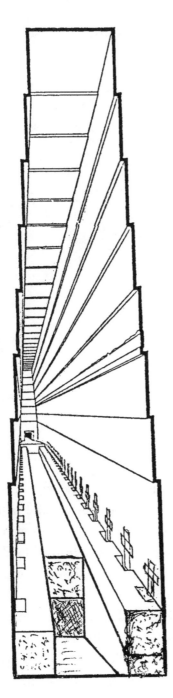

Figure 42

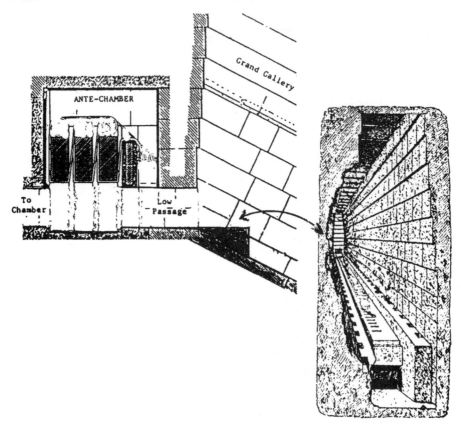

Figure 43

to him a ladder; he climbed up, spoke to them, looked around, and climbed back down. All is ready for you, he said; we were to use this ladder to climb up to where the workmen were, and then we would continue farther up by means of additional ladders; it had to be done one at a time, he explained, because the ledge and the way up from it are narrow. And then he left.

It looked like a flimsy and unsafe arrangement to me; so Wally volunteered to go up first. After Wally climbed from the ledge up the next ladder, Abbas went up, and called out to me from the ledge, encouraging me to follow. As he turned to climb farther up, I reached for the ladder and was about to take the first step up. At that moment I suddenly felt a mighty blow to my head: A large and heavy piece of wood, dropped from higher up, hit me smack on my head and knocked me down. Warm blood began to pour down from the top of my head, and I was certain that my skull had been cracked.

I cried out in pain. Abbas, back on the ledge, shouted to me: What happened? "My skull is cracked, I am bleeding!" I shouted. He climbed down, grabbed hold of me, and half supporting, half carrying me as I staggered, rushed me out to our car, ordering his manager to drive back to the hotel. There's a doctor there, he said. The handkerchief I was holding to my head was soaking with blood; blood was spilling on my clothing. I was sure it was my end, and myriad thoughts of finality raced through my mind.

It took forever—so it seemed to me—to reach the hotel clinic. The doctor, American trained and speaking English, examined me, cleaned the wound, and bandaged it. I think it's just superficial, he said, the blow just cut the skin on your head; but it's advisable to take X-rays and make sure there is no internal concussion. Also, he said, you need a Tetanus shot, since what hit you could have been infected. He advised Abbas to take me to a hospital without delay.

We returned to the lobby, where the anxious local manager of Abbas was waiting. Steadier and less apprehensive, I asked for a cup of coffee. We sat down to evaluate the situation. I kept asking Abbas what had happened, who dropped the piece of wood on me. He said he didn't know; it was an accident. Was it? I said—it had nothing to do with the newspaper article? I don't think I am safe in Egypt, I said. I think I'd better get back to New York right away, I told Abbas—*tonight.*

Where is Wally? I asked. He must have stayed behind in the Pyramid, Abbas said. Ask him if he would rather stay one more day as originally scheduled or come with me tonight, if there are seats on the flight, I said to Abbas.

His manager inquired and said there's a hospital nearby; he could take me to it. It seemed advisable to let them take a look, at least get the recommended Tetanus shot. I left with him for the hospital, while Abbas was going to deal with the flight arrangements. Getting the Tetanus shot was no simple matter, but I'll skip details of the experience.

When we returned to the hotel, Wally was there; he had already heard what happened to me. His hand was bandaged; What happened to YOU? I inquired. He leaned toward me and said in a whisper: I tried to break off a piece of stone with red ink markings on it, and all I managed to do was to cut myself. He too could not explain how the piece of wood dropped—or was dropped—on me. Told of my plan to leave tonight, he said he'd come with me.

We discussed again the day's events. In spite of Abbas's assurances that it was just an accident, I kept feeling it was deliberate. Does Hawass know what happened? I asked. For sure, Abbas said—I am sure it was reported to him. So why did he not call me to find out how I am? I asked—after all, I came here this time by his invitation, in a manner of speaking. Maybe he intended to call you tomorrow, Abbas said. I wonder, I said, shaking my aching head in doubt.

As I rested in my room until it was time to leave, I kept thinking about the day's events. Without a close examination of the markings, without photographs, with no red-paint sample, was anything achieved?

Later that evening we left for the airport. From the hotel we could see the searchlights and hear the music of the nightly Sound and Light show up the hill at Giza. It seemed quite ironic to me:

At the end of my Fateful Day—the day I almost got killed inside the Great Pyramid—I was leaving empty handed; and the Great Pyramid, defiant, continued to keep its secrets.

5

OOPS IN THE CAIRO MUSEUM

The Egyptian Museum is the depository of Egypt's archaeological heritage—the place to which its archaeological finds, once discovered and moved, come for safekeeping, study, and display. Until its current ongoing expansion and renovation, it had been a pastel-colored two-storied building erected in 1900 in a quiet Cairo neighborhood—only to find itself by the end of the twentieth century in the city's bustling center, bursting to the rafters with more than 100,000 archaeological artifacts.

By the time I acted there as guide for my first Expedition group in 1994, I had become quite familiar with the Museum, its layout, and its exhibits from previous visits, starting in the 1980s; but my first virtual visit to it took place in 1971—in New York City, when the Metropolitan Museum of Art held the special exhibit "Treasures of Egyptian Art from the Cairo Museum." It was indeed, as advertised, a unique exhibit, for it was the first time that the most important sculpture artifacts of the Egyptian Museum were sent abroad on such a comprehensive scale.

The exhibit's catalogue had on its cover a photograph of a famous and precious stone sculpture—that of the Pharaoh Chefren seated on a majestic throne and protected by the falcon-god Horus (fig. 44). It was a choice justified not only by the antiquity and artistic quality of

Figure 44

the artifact; since Chefren/Chefra is considered by Egyptologists to have been the builder of the Second Pyramid of Giza, the photographic choice was appropriate because the Giza pyramids are ancient Egypt's best-known monuments.

Appropriate too was the next large stone sculpture on exhibit, that of the Pharaoh Mycerinus/Menkaura in divine company (fig. 45), for

Figure 45

he was—was he not?—the presumed builder of the Third Pyramid in Giza and of the even more famous Sphinx. The two sculptures are imposing in size: That of the seated Chefren a massive 5.5 feet in height, and that of the standing Mycerinus over 3 feet in height—sizes befitting the sizes of the pyramids attributed to them. One could thus expect—as I did—to find an even more impressive large statue of

Khufu/Cheops, builder of the even grander Great Pyramid; ***but there was none.***

Was it missing because there was no statue of Khufu, the greatest builder of them all? I found the answer when I actually visited the Museum in Cairo. Yes, there is a statue—one sole carved image—of Cheops/Khufu; but it is not an imposing one as would befit the builder of the greatest stone edifice on Earth; it is a tiny statuette, carved of ivory, less than 3 *inches* high (fig. 46). It was a shame to bring it over to New York (and Boston and Los Angeles, where the special exhibit was also shown). The curators, both in the USA and in Egypt, did not need the embarrassment of an OOP.

"OOP" is an acronym, the initials of "**O**ut **O**f **P**lace"—a term applied to archaeological objects that do not belong to the period, the place, the culture in which they were found. There are true OOP artifacts—physical objects whose existence cannot be denied, yet they

Figure 46

are "cannot be" objects that could not possibly exist; they are by any yardstick Out Of Place. Other OOPs are categorized as such because they make the experts feel that they "do not belong" simply because they do not conform to the Establishment's tenets. And then there are OOPs which, for one reason or another, are just embarrassing—if it were up to the experts, they should not have been found at all; but here they are!

Whatever the OOP category, they pose a problem to the museum authorities: What shall be done with such embarrassing objects? Various museums deal variably with the OOP problem. Without doubt, more than a few such objects end up just out of sight, never displayed, and probably as often as not remaining unknown.

An example of that is the case of the Headless Spaceman (fig. 47), an artifact that the Istanbul Museum in Turkey has refrained from displaying because "there were no astronauts and spacecraft 4,500 years ago." For five decades the Museum even denied the existence of the artifact. When I was tipped off about it in the 1990s, I was visiting Turkey as a guest of the Turkish Government, so the Museum could not deny the object's existence, but explained its non-display by its being a fake. It finally put it on display under my persistence; but then removed it again . . .

Readers of the first book of *The Earth Chronicles Expeditions* will also recall the case of the Olmec elephant toy (fig. 48) that was on display in the Jalapa Museum in Mexico, and then was removed (together with a wall panel dating the Olmec civilization to ca. 3000 B.C.)—undoubtedly because of its embarrassing proof that Africans (familiar with elephants that do not exist in the Americas) somehow arrived in Mesoamerica thousands of years before Columbus, when people could not possibly cross the Atlantic Ocean.

Figure 47

Figure 48

The Egyptian Museum in Cairo too has its embarrassing OOPs; the diminutive Cheops statuette has been one of them, and was treated accordingly . . .

***

Some museums arrange their exhibits chronologically; others by category, or by provenance, or by the "culture" to which they belong. The Egyptian Museum chose to display its artifacts by the period to which they belonged—Old Kingdom, Middle Kingdom, New Kingdom—and their dynasties.

Thus, as one entered the Museum (Room 48 in the ground-level floor plan, fig. 49) looking for the Old Kingdom's famed kings, the statue of Menkaura was encountered to the left in room 47; the statue of Chefra who preceded him was placed farther back in room 42, next to a large limestone statue of **Zoser** from Sakkara.

And where is **Khufu**/Cheops? His embarrassing statuette is nowhere to be seen in this Old Kingdom section. It is not even on the ground floor. And unless one knows exactly where to look on the second floor, it will be missed altogether; for it has been placed up there, along

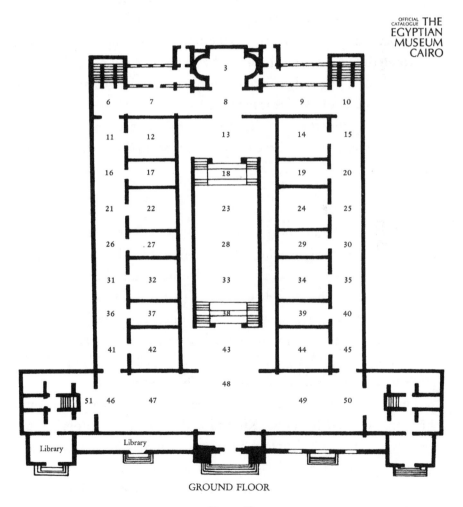

OFFICIAL CATALOGUE THE
EGYPTIAN
MUSEUM
CAIRO

GROUND FLOOR

Figure 49

with other knickknacks, in a glass-covered tabletop display case near the stairs leading down and out of the Museum. The main attraction on that second floor of the Museum are the dazzling finds from the tomb of Tutankhamen, of the New Kingdom's Eighteenth Dynasty, including his golden death mask (plate 15); but visitors uninformed of the little Khufu, just walk by and go down the stairs.

Once, visiting the Museum with my Expedition group, I left the group to linger at the Tutankhamen displays (I had seen those artifacts several times before), and found a chair to sit on next to the Khufu-containing display case. Waiting for the group to reach the stairs to go back down (at which time I was going to show them the statuette), I was contemplating not so much the statuette itself as its location. I was in fact wondering: No matter the size, why have the Museum's officials not granted a chronologically correct and a deserved place of honor to the presumed builder of the Great Pyramid?

Could it be that in their innermost hearts they too have doubts?

And that leads us to the second Cairo Museum OOP, the Inventory Stela.

***

The Egyptian Museum was established in 1858 by the French archaeologist Auguste Mariette, whom many consider the Father of modern Egyptology, mostly with archaeological objects that he himself had unearthed; the Inventory Stela was one of them. He found it in Giza in 1853, in the remains of a temple for the goddess Isis situated beside the Great Pyramid and the Sphinx—exactly where according to the stela's inscription (see fig. 13, page 17) it was set up by Cheops/Khufu: In the temple beside the *already existing* Great Pyramid and Sphinx.

The Inventory Stela was so named because, after the opening lines which we have quoted earlier, Khufu listed on it an "inventory" of the religious objects that he had found in the Isis temple when he undertook its restoration. He does make reference to a small pyramid *which he says he built* to honor the princess Henutsen (whom he married?)—one of the three small pyramids at the eastern foot of the Great Pyramid (see figs. 5 and 6, pages 7 and 8). Would he not have claimed to having also built the Great Pyramid were he its builder?

As earlier explained, the Inventory Stela was irrefutable proof, provided by Khufu/Cheops himself, that *he did not build* the Great Pyramid, and that the Pyramid (and Sphinx) were already there in his time. Although that created a problem for Egyptologists committed to the Khufu-built-it tenet, the artifact could not be hidden away—it was found, after all, by the Museum's very founder, and its discovery was reported in the scientific journals of the time, which also printed a picture of it (fig. 50). So what could archaeologists do with such an OOP? They declared it to be a forgery, perpetrated (at a later time) by the ancient Egyptians themselves!

Not all the Egyptologists of the early twentieth century were doubters. James H. Breasted *(Ancient Records of Egypt)* felt that the Inventory Stela bore all the marks of authenticity and included it in the list of Fourth Dynasty artifacts. The great French Egyptologist Gaston Maspero *(The Dawn of Civilization)* suggested that even if it was from a later time, it was a copy of an earlier authentic artifact, and thus a factual record of the life and deeds of Khufu.

But considerations of national pride—led in the 1930s by a foremost native Egyptologist, Selim Hassan—finally dominated the purely scientific discussions. In the words of Hassan *(Excavations at Giza)*, the inscription was made "long after the death of Khufu" but its makers invoked his name "to support some fictitious claim of the local priests." The suggested "long after" date was that of the Twenty-sixth Saitic Dynasty—an incredible two thousand years later! But, heeding Hassan's nationalistic views, the Stela was moved to the very back of the Museum's ground floor, placed in a row with other stelas from such later periods.

Some fifty years later, on my first visit to the Egyptian Museum in Cairo, I went to that back area of the ground floor to see the Stela; but I couldn't find it. I asked the guards about it, showing them the illustration that I had with me; but they had no idea what I was talking about. I asked to talk to the Curator, or anyone else in the Director's office. It was not a simple matter, but I managed to get someone there to talk to

Figure 50

me. Grudgingly looking up the Museum directory and other lists, the person said Yes, the Stela is there, in the back row. I went back, but still couldn't find it. Back at the Director's office, they told me, in so many words, to stop bothering them.

In all subsequent visits I made sure to look for the Inventory Stela; but I could not find it. In the Briefing Notes I prepared for the first

Earth Chronicles Expedition group, I listed the Inventory Stela among the "must see" artifacts and included its photograph, asking all in the group to try and find it—anywhere in the Museum.

But this OOP is still missing.

***

There has been another OOP—a true OOP—that has fared better in Cairo's Egyptian Museum. For the sake of identification, I will call it "The Flywheel," though what it really is remains an enigma.

The best way to describe it is to show a picture of it—an actual photograph (plate 16). It was discovered in 1936 in the tomb of the crown prince Sabu, son of king Adjib of the *First Dynasty,* in northern Sakkara—just south of Giza. It is thus certain that the object was placed in the tomb circa 3100 B.C.; so the object as such must be at least that old, but could of course be older.

Reporting this and other discoveries in that tomb and others near it, Walter B. Emery *(Great Tombs of the First Dynasty)* described the object as a "bowl-like vessel of schist" and remarked that "No satisfactory explanation of the curious design of this object has been forthcoming."

The object is indeed curious, unusual, *and unique.* Round—some twenty-four inches in diameter—it has three precise curved cutouts that create three complex bladelike surfaces. A central hole, with a protruding rim, suggests that the object was made to fit over an axle, probably for rotation purposes. A thin circular frame surrounds these features; and the whole thing looks extremely delicate—it is less than four inches at its thickest (fig. 51). The shape and curvatures suggested to technical experts that the object was intended to be immersed in some liquid.

Materials studies revealed that the object was carved out of a solid block of schist—a rock which is very brittle and which easily splits into thin irregular layers. That such a stone was chosen suggests that it was nevertheless used because only it made possible the elegantly precise shaping of the object's unusual curved parts and cutouts. But the experts who examined it doubted whether the object, if it were put into actual rotational use, could have remained intact for long, if at all—it would

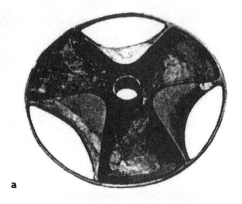

a

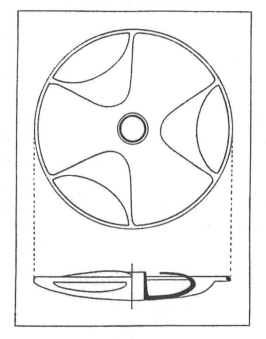

b

Figure 51

have quickly split apart under the centrifugal force. This has led some, like Cyril Aldred *(Egypt to the End of the Old Kingdom),* to conclude that the stone object "Possibly imitates a form originally made of metal."

According to such opinions, this was a *stone copy* of a functional *metal* object. But the only metal in use by people 5,000 or more years ago was copper, and to cast the object out of copper required a mold even more complex than the object itself. Was it then somehow machined to obtain its complex and delicate shape? If so—with which precision tools?

This last question applies whether the stone object is a copy of a metal original or the actual original itself. But apart from the questions of how the object was made, or of what material, there remain the basic puzzling questions: What was it for? If it was rotating on an axle, what was the axle attached to or part of? Who had the technical ability to make it—and who had the technology that needed it and used it?

The object's possible function occurred to me some forty years after its discovery, as I was reading in a technical journal about a revolution-ary design of a *flywheel* that a California-based company was developing for the American space program. A flywheel, it needs to be explained, is a circular wheel-like object attached to the rotating shaft of a machine or an engine as a means to regulate the equipment's speed of rotation—or (as in metal presses, vehicles such as trains or buses, or in aviation) to store energy for power surges.

The flywheel has been in use for more than two centuries; its basic mechanical property has been the ability to store in the flywheel's cir-cumference the energy obtained in the center—for which reason, the circumference had to be solidly thick and heavy. But in the 1970s engi-neers of the Lockheed Missile & Space Company developed an opposite design—with a lightweight rimmed wheel (fig. 52a). Their research was continued by the Airesearch Manufacturing Company which developed a light-rimmed flywheel, hermetically sealed so that it could be used while immersed in a housing *filled with a lubricating liquid.* Responding to my request, Airesearch sent me photographs of their flywheel (fig. 52b) with a portfolio of technical data, which strengthened my guess that the ancient object was some kind of a flywheel of advanced design—storing the energy in a thin rim and rotating in a lubricating liquid.

Since the Egyptians of 3100 B.C. (or earlier) did not have the tech-nology to manufacture the object, or the sophisticated equipment in which it could be used, the "Flywheel" was clearly an OOP. Nevertheless, the Museum authorities did not hide it away in a basement corner; they did put it on display—as far as I recall, in Room 43 among other small

FLYWHEELS

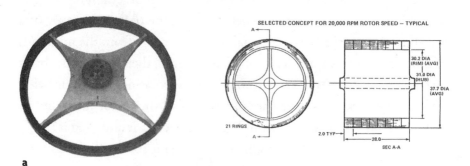

a

b

Figure 52

finds from the earliest dynasties. The logic behind the decision to display this object, I assume, was that if the early Pharaohs could build the Giza Pyramids, why wouldn't they possess other sophisticated capabilities? Unlike the Inventory Stela, it—according to this logic—affirmed rather than contradicted the "Our ancestors could do it!" stance.

But of course, if you ***doubt*** one, you cannot help but doubt the other . . .

***

Since the "Flywheel" irrefutably exists, and since it must be dated to 3100 B.C. or earlier, the basic questions remain: Who could have manufactured it, to what kind of advanced technological equipment was it attached, and who made and used such advanced equipment?

Plate 1. The Great Pyramid

Plate 2. The Sphinx with the two pyramids in the background

Plate 3. Cleaned up Niche in the Great Pyramid's Queen's Chamber,
also showing southern shaft opening

Plate 4. Niche opening covered with wire-mesh frame

Plate 5. Different Niche opening, February 1995

Plate 6. Niche opening: cover removed, looking in

Plate 8. Cogswell emerging from the passageway

Plate 7. Cogswell's flashlight shining from inside the secret passageway

Plate 9. Photograph from inside the passageway, looking back toward the entryway

Plate 10. Photograph taken near the entrance to the secret chamber (note the blackened lintel stone)

Plate 12. The upper part of the chamber and its blackened ceiling

Plate 11. Looking into the secret chamber

Plate 13. The chamber's walls and some of its ceiling stones

Plate 14. The tunnel's stonework, approaching the exit

Plate 15. Gold mask of Tutankhamen

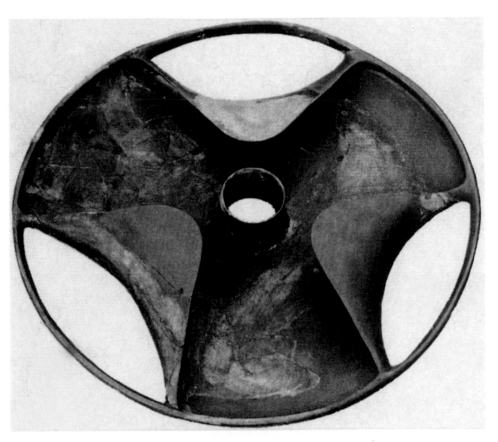

Plate 16. "Flywheel" from 3100 B.C.

Plate 17. Earth Chronicles Expedition group at Stonehenge

Plate 18. Ggantija, the largest temple on the island of Gozo

Plate 19. View of Hagar Qim temple on Malta

Plate 20. Earth Chronicles Expedition group dwarfed by
boulders at Hagar Qim

Plate 21. Tarxien temple

Plate 22. Expedition group photo of Sun's rays on the marker stone in the
Mnajdra lower temple on Summer Solstice

Plate 23.
Malta ruts

Plate 24. Malta
ruts at
"Clapham
Junction"

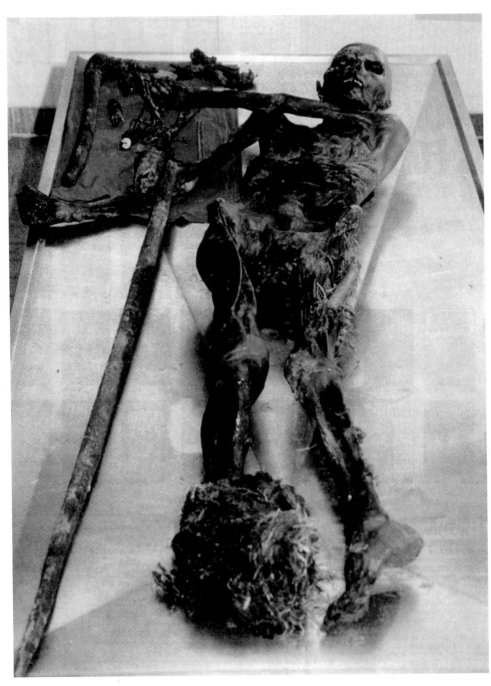

Plate 25. The Iceman of the Alps at the Archaeological Museum of South Tyrol in Bolzano, Italy

Plate 26. Statue of Ptah

Plate 27. The Shroud of Turin on display

Plate 28. Leonardo da Vinci's *The Last Supper*

Plate 29. The author with Monsignor Balducci

Plate 30. *Creation of Adam*, Sistine Chapel

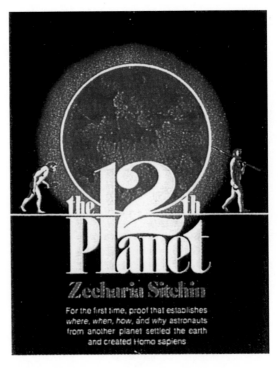

Plate 31. *The 12th Planet* original cover

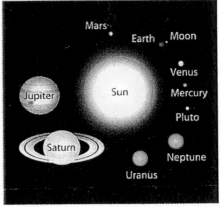

Plate 32. The two illustrations from the sidebar of the
Sky & Telescope article

Plate 33. The main part of the Antikythera Mechanism

Plate 34. Remains of Harran's medieval defensive walls

Plate 35. Jacob's well in Harran

Plate 36. Harran temple ruins

Plate 37. The author with Nabuna'id stela

Plate 38. The "Candelabra" carved into a mountainside in the Bay of Paracas on Peru's coast northwest of Tiahuanacu

Plate 39. View of Puma Punku

Plate 40. Precisely cut stones at Puma Punku

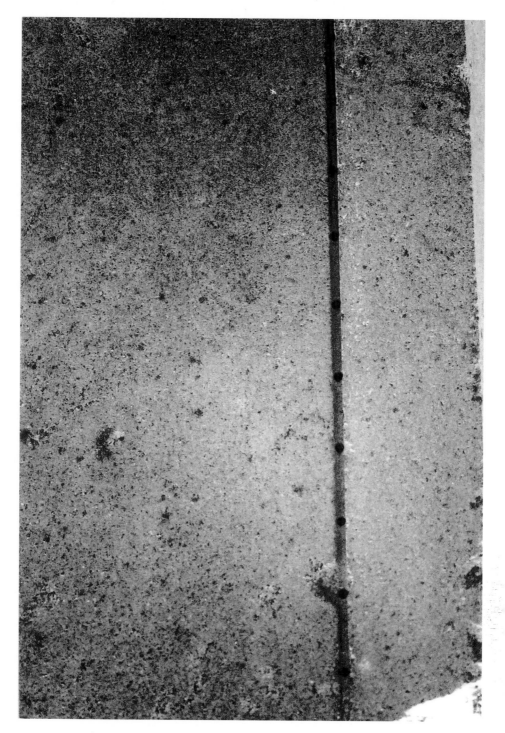

Plate 41. Grooves for gold nails for gold-plated walls, Puma Punku

Plate 42. Complex cut stones at Puma Punku

Plate 43. Complex cut stones at Puma Punku

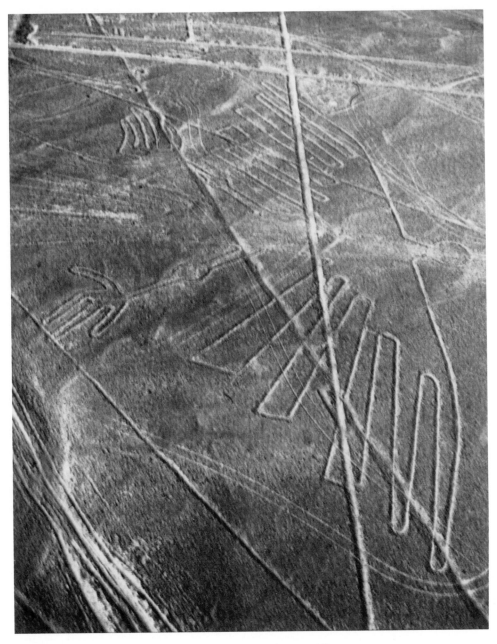

Plate 44. Nazca Lines with animal figure

Plate 45. Nazca Lines with animal figure

Plate 46. Straight-running Nazca Lines

Plate 47. Intriguing circular markings in the mountains not far from the Nazca Lines in Peru

Plate 48. Intriguing circular markings in the mountains not far from the Nazca Lines

I dare give one answer to all three questions: The gods.

In *The Stairway to Heaven* I provided information about ancient Egypt's oldest center of worship, the city of **An** (the biblical On), later known as Heliopolis. In its great temple, one of the "Celestial Chambers" in which the gods arrived on Earth, was kept an object called the *Ben-Ben*. We can surmise how the temple, called Het Ben-Ben ("Sacred House of the Ben-Ben"), looked from its hieroglyphic pictograph, which in time also served as the hieroglyphic sign for the city's name: A rocket's launch tower (fig. 53). We also know how the Ben-Ben itself looked, because a stone model of it was found (fig. 54a). Akin to a modern command capsule of an astronauts' rocketship (fig. 54b), the discovered stone model even depicts its occupant peering out through an open hatch-door.

Figure 53

a

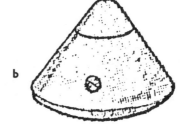
b

Figure 54

In this temple the Ben-Ben and other space-travel paraphernalia were not only kept—they were displayed and opened for view, by the king, in a special annual ceremony intended to remind the people of the gods' space origins. The *Het Ben-Ben* and its contents are long gone. How and when the temple was ruined and its contents gone, no one knows; but it has occurred to me that the "Flywheel" might have been one of the objects originally kept in that ancient "Smithsonian Institution."

Let this thought be with you if you go to Cairo and look for the enigmatic OOPs.

6

ENIGMAS MADE OF STONE

W hy are Earthlings fascinated by the heavens?

I asked the question, and gave an answer, in my 1993 book *When Time Began*. I did so in the context of astronomical computers made of stone—the best known of which is Stonehenge in England. Found in Europe, in the Near East, in the Americas (and possibly also in the Far East), they all inexplicably linked observations of the Sun and the Moon to an artificial division of the heavens into twelve parts called the Zodiac. I suggested that the key to unlocking the secrets and enigmas they posed lay in recognizing that they were a product of the technologies of the gods, not of Man—that they were designed by a Divine Architect.

The records of Earthlings' fascination with the heavens permeate the halls of the British Museum in London, a modern Temple of Knowledge dedicated to Mankind's history, civilizations, and (unavoidably) gods. During the decades of my research for my writings, there were many times when I had spent two-week stretches of stay in London (my alma mater having been the London School of Economics and Political Science), devoting daily long hours to the British Museum's exhibits and famed round Library.

It was there that I could study in the Library about the Mesopotamian Epic of Creation, and then see the actual seven clay tablets of *Enuma elish*—a text treated by scholars as an allegorical tale of celestial gods, but which in fact constitutes a sophisticated cosmogony scientifically describing our Solar System, the origins of the Earth, and of life upon it. It was there that I could read (in the Library) about the Anunnaki gods and their coming to Earth, then see (among the exhibits) an amazing circular tablet (see chapter 10) whose eight segments deal with the gods' space journeys from their planet (Nibiru) to Earth.

It was in the British Museum that I could read about and then see an astronomical tablet, divided into columns and filled with numbers which, when rendered into modern characters, was revealed to simulate a computer printout of data ***predicting lunar eclipses fifty years in advance.*** And it was there that I could see for myself, then peruse in voluminous writings, the evidence about ***the ancient zodiacal knowledge***—familiarity with a phenomenon that causes one group of stars to replace another, at sunrise, once in about 2,100 years. In one Mesopotamian artifact after another, references to those twelve (fig. 55) constellations and their depictions (fig. 56) were omnipresent.

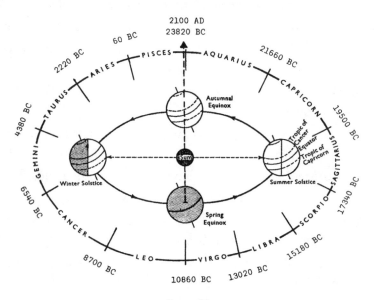

Figure 55

Figure 56

But it was when I went to visit Stonehenge for the first time, and stood there inside the circle of stones that had been brought from far away (as has been the case in megalithic structures all over the world), that the question popped up in my head: WHY has Mankind, why have Earthlings, been so fascinated with the heavens—and gone to immense lengths to observe them?

The familiar view of Stonehenge with its columns (fig. 57) is just the current stage of its varied phases, going back to the third millennium B.C. Stonehenge, all researchers agree, functioned throughout its various stages (fig. 58) as a ***device to determine the Zodiacal Age*** by observing sunrise on Summer Solstice Day, the sightline reextending from the so-called **Altar Stone** in the center, through two determining pillars, via the **Avenue,** to the so-called **Heel Stone** farther out (fig. 59a).

Sir Norman Lockyer, the father of Archaeoastronomy, used Stone-henge *(Stonehenge and Other British Stone Monuments)* to illustrate how the solstice view line helps determine when the structure was built. This is so because the solstice point is determined by the Earth's

Figure 57

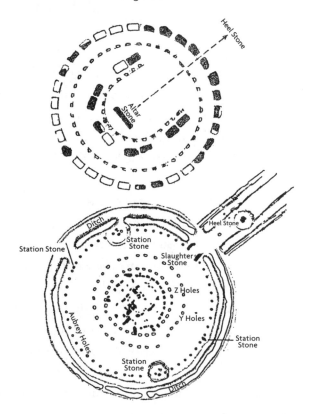

Figure 58

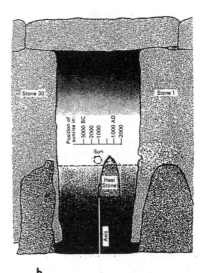

a   b

Figure 59

tilt-angle ("inclination") relative to its orbital path ("the Ecliptic"). This tilt changes over the ages as the Earth slightly wobbles—for example, from 24.11° in 4000 B.C. to 23.92° in 2000 B.C. to about 23.5° nowadays. The original view line to the Heel Stone matched the inclination circa 2100 B.C. when the Zodiacal Age was shifting from Taurus to Aries.

In the four thousand years since then, this view line no longer correctly points to the then prevailing zodiacal constellations; one can indeed see that the axis is nowadays misaligned even though the Heel Stone had been moved (fig. 59b). Nevertheless, Summer Solstice Day— June 21—is a big thing at Stonehenge. Believers dressed as Druid priests perform ritual dances, and multitudes gather there to view at dawn the Sun rise between the two guiding pillars, no matter which star constellation is seen in the partly darkened horizon.

In its heyday, some have concluded, Stonehenge also served as a predictor of *lunar phenomena,* as the ground markings of a rectangular arrangement suggests (fig. 60). The Boston University mathematician and astronomer Gerald Hawkins *(Stonehenge Decoded),* who described Stonehenge as an astronomical predictor, was fascinated by the number 19 that the stones and place-holes in the various circles expressed, and

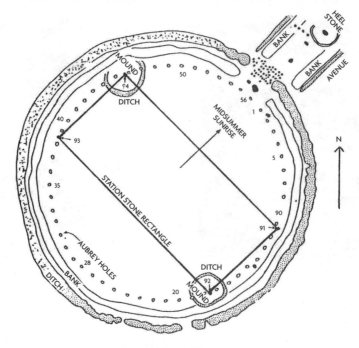

Figure 60

deemed it an unmistakable application of the ***Metonic Cycle*** (the cycle of 235 lunar months in the Moon-Earth-Sun orbital relationships).

Such an aspect of Stonehenge, though relating to a cycle of only 19 years (compared to the 2,100 years of the zodiacal shift), is nevertheless an indication of high astronomical sophistication, since the complex Earth-Sun-Moon relationship underlies the phenomena of not only lunar but also ***solar eclipses;*** and predicting them was of immense religious and political importance.

The June 1999 Earth Chronicles Expedition (to England and Malta) began in London with repeat visits to the British Museum (facilitated by staying at a hotel virtually next door to it). It was a necessary prelude, I felt, to the subsequent visit to Stonehenge—a visit timed with Solstice Day in mind. By special arrangement our group was allowed into the monument's stone circle early in the morning, before regular visiting time, to provide us with an hour by ourselves (plate 17). We walked about, looked for the various markers, checked the view lines. Many lay down on the ground among the monoliths, trying to get some feeling, inspiration, vibration, or whatever by the direct contact with the earth. We left with a sense of awe and wonderment: Here, without doubt, was a great monument from the past—built by men, but conceived by some greater knowing mind.

The tour included other astronomically significant Neolithic ("New Stone Age") sites in the area, such as Silbury Hill and the large Avebury Circle (fig. 61); a bonus was an unplanned sighting of a fresh Crop Circle that appeared nearby the night before, joining previous ones in the same vicinity (fig. 62).

But it all took place two days ahead of Solstice Day, to avoid the crush of people; I chose to let my group witness the actual everlasting celestial phenomenon in the relatively uncrowded island of Malta, the Expedition's next destination.

Figure 61

Figure 62

***

The Mediterranean Sea is bounded by three continents—Europe, Asia, and Africa. The island of Malta, together with the island of Sicily and neighboring smaller islands, undoubtedly once formed a physical geographic landbridge connecting the continents. After the waters surged (was it the biblical Great Flood?) and sea level rose, Malta—now an island—has continued to serve as a cultural bridge not only between North and South, but also between East and West. Migrants, settlers, seafarers, conquerors—from the most ancient times through the Phoenicians and the Romans, Moslems and Crusaders (the famed Knights of Malta), and World War II warriors—all left their mark there.

Nevertheless—or perhaps because of that—Malta's enigmas remain unsolved puzzles. All those settlers, visitors, and conquerors from far larger lands (Malta and its two small satellite islands, Gozo and Comino, represent an area of just 122 square miles!) and their civilizations cannot explain Malta's two main mysteries: *Its stone "Temples" and the "Ruts."*

"Temples" is a term applied by locals and scholars to structures when their real purpose is unknown; and in an odd way I became aware of Malta's ones long before I ever went there. One reason was an elderly gentleman by name of Joseph Ellul, who started to write to me after he had read *The 12th Planet*. He claimed that his family had lived on the island for 500 years and owned the land where one of the best preserved temples was situated; he therefore knew all about the temples since childhood and wrote books in which he identified descendants of the biblical Noah as the builders of Malta's temples. Another was the Society for the Research and Investigation of Phenomena, headquartered in Malta's capital, Valletta, which invited me to come, give a lecture, and find out the "Maltese connection" in support of my writings.

In 1999 I finally went to Malta. The Society no longer functioned, but Mr. Ellul was still there, eagerly awaiting my arrival. Among the advice he showered on us was one most practical: Where best to watch sunrise on Solstice Day and how to reach and enter the temple ahead of the anticipated crowd . . .

***

The temples and their sites dot the two main islands, Malta and Gozo (fig. 63). They are constructed of megalithic stone boulders, and their most distinct or obvious feature is their shape (fig. 64). In all of them, the shape follows an unusual yet distinctive pattern that suggests a preconceived architectural concept (or purpose). They are neither square nor rectangular—as temples everywhere else are—but consist of a series of oval-like or elliptical chambers ("apses"), arranged as "cloverleafs," within

Figure 63

a larger perimeter delineated by an outer wall that also forms an oval. They occupy sizeable areas, and were sometimes built as twins—two "cloverleaf" temples rising side by side—a feature that has led some to see therein an underlying religious concept of Duality.

Typical both of the oval shapes, cloverleaf layouts and the twinlike "duality" is the largest temple of them all, the one at Ggantija (pronounced Jeguntiya) on the island of Gozo (plate 18). Dramatically situated on a promontory overlooking the bay, its two parts or twin temples each have their separate entranceway, with one oval chamber or enclosure connected by a short passageway to another "lobed" cloverleaf enclosure; but there are no connecting corridors or other passages between the two twin parts; so why are the two adjoining?

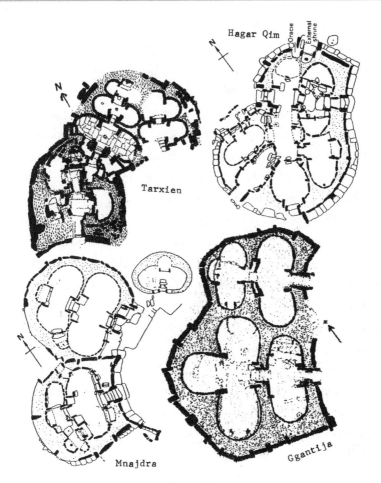

Figure 64

At the nearby site of Xaghra on Gozo the cloverleaf "duality" also prevails; so do the remains of the temple at Mnajdra (pronounced Mnaidra) on Malta proper. But at the site called Tarxien (pronounced Tarshen), the temple's remains include—in addition to the twinlike cloverleafs—a series of oval enclosures and undefined structures that might have been cloverleaf chambers. And at the best preserved site on Malta, Hagar Qim (pronounced Hajar Im) there is a series of four oval chambers arranged in a semicircle in addition to the recognizable cloverleafs.

The number of cloverleaf chambers, it would thus appear, cannot support "duality" or such other religious theories. Yet, the proponents of "those were temples" notions hold that the inner layouts of these structures confirm their religious functions. The concave shape of the walls at the main entranceways, they say, created a forecourt for assembly and the bringing of sacrificial animals; the convex or semi-oval "lobe" chamber at the inner end, they explain, was a kind of an inner sanctum, a Holy of Holies. At least in one place that we have visited, two stone columns flanking the access to such an innermost section had cut-through holes in them which in all probability (we actually tried it!) enabled ropes to hold up a screen that could be moved up and down; so maybe the enclosure was indeed a particularly sacred section. Doorways, doorposts, niches, small raised platforms—all of stone—have been called altars, prayer alcoves, sacrifice tables, oracle posts, etc., etc., in line with the "temple" concept.

If so, which deity was worshipped there, and by whom?

A religious purpose in these designs, that are repeated in all of the still standing temple complexes, seems to be confirmed by the discovery (in several of them) of stone sculptures of a fat—very fat—female with exaggerated (some even use the term "elephantine" to describe the size) feminine parts (fig. 65). She is assumed to have been a goddess—a "Mother Goddess" image that was presumably worshipped as a fertility deity. The similarity of the architectural design of the temples to her rounded features (fig. 66) strikes one as soon as these statues are viewed in the National Museum of Archaeology in Valletta, Malta's capital. The assumption is that the structures were shaped in the image of the goddess and served as temples where she was worshipped; but in the absence of writing of any kind, nothing about her or her cult is known.

Who were the worshippers—the presumed builders of these temples? It is generally assumed that the first settlers in Malta arrived from the nearby island of Sicily (less than 60 miles away), in the fifth millennium B.C. In the third millennium B.C. new settlers—farmers, this time—came from the somewhat farther islands of Sardinia and Corsica, bringing with them domestic animals. Did any of them build the temples? That is a tricky question, because the answer depends on dating these structures.

Figure 65

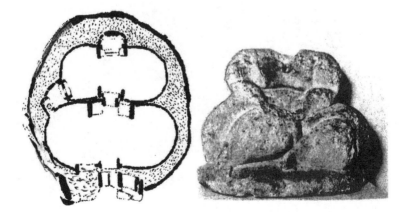

Figure 66

In spite of the similarities of the various temples, even the casual visitor can discern great differences between them. The ones deemed the earliest, on the island of Gozo, are constructed of boulders that were found in the local area. Megalithic stones, only some of them smoothed and shaped (as in the Ggantija temple) were selectively placed as gateways; otherwise, the fieldstones were just piled up to form walls and partitions. By comparison, the Hagar Qim temple on Malta proper (fig. 67) has long sections of walls constructed of immense natural boulders (plate 19) that dwarfed our group (plate 20), other walls of only dressed stone blocks, still others of mixtures of natural boulders with cut and shaped stone blocks, and partitions made of great stone blocks purposely shaped with openings cut through them. And the complex Tarxien temple—deemed the latest in the series—has almost modern-looking sections and geometric-design decorations (plate 21).

The various temples began to be excavated in the 1820s and for more than a century thereafter archaeologists deemed the Temple Building Period to have run from circa 2800 B.C. (Ggantija) to 2400 B.C. (Tarxien). Later studies based on the availability of carbon dating reduced the antiquity to circa 2450 and 2100 B.C., respectively—the 2100 B.C. date being the firmest, since something unknown caused an abrupt interruption of the island's habitation after that.

Figure 67

The construction of these temples even at those dates—it is estimated that there may have been about forty of them—is a great technological achievement. Although the islands' small size rules out the hauling of the large and heavy stone boulders from very great distances (as has been the case in so many other places in both the Old and the New Worlds), just obtaining the boulders, transporting them to the site, dressing, shaping and decorating many of them, lifting them, and emplacing them in the planned positions, required substantial efforts, an organized society, architectural and structural knowledge, and some kind of technology that no one has been able to truly figure out. Although the above dates correspond not only to the Copper Age but already the Bronze Age in the eastern Mediterranean, no such metal tools were discovered in the Maltese sites; only flint knives and obsidian tools were found in the temples.

The puzzle was then magnified by new claims that some of the temples were already standing and functioning before 3800 B.C.

The claims, which in time found their way into most brochures about Malta by starting its description with the words that "its stone temples predate Stonehenge and even the pyramids of Egypt," began in the 1970s when the archaeologist J. D. Evans *(The Prehistoric Antiquities of the Maltese Islands)* pointed out that the lower or southernmost temple in Mnajdra appears to have an axis oriented to the east, which would make it a Solar Temple. This was followed by the application, in the 1980s, of Lockyer's archaeoastronomy methods to the Malta temples—specifically, to Mnajdra—by two Maltese experts, Paul Micaleff and Alfred Xuereb. Micaleff reported their findings in his 1989 book *Mnajdra Prehistoric Temple.* The lower temple at Mnajdra, they concluded, was "a calendar in stone," built precisely to view the equinoxes and solstices (fig. 68).

Based on geographic position, the site's elevation, and the Azimuth that indicates true north, they figured that the portal for the Sun's rays was built when the Earth's Declination Angle was just under 24.1°. Using Lockyer's system to determine the date of construction by the angle of declination, they arrived at the date of 3710 B.C. Since the other temples,

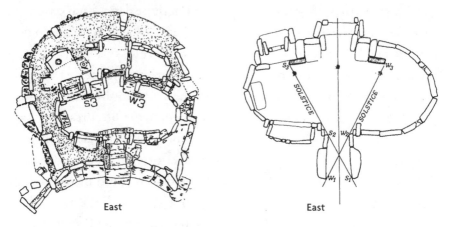

East   East

Figure 68

such as the Ggantija one, were built hundreds of years earlier—the claim for Malta's "First" in the construction of stone temples followed.

This, I must say, sounded far-fetched to me. The dwellers in Malta at that early period were engaged in primitive farming and used stone tools; could they have performed the technological feats ascribed to them? On close examination, it turned out that the photographic evidence in Micaleff's book, of the sunray shining on a particular stone, was taken not on Solstice Day but on Equinox Day; it confirmed the orientation of that particular axis to the East—but not more than that.

***

And so it was that early on ***Summer Solstice Day*** in 1999 I and my Expeditions group set out not only to view sunrise—but also to check out the feasibility of the fourth millennium B.C. dates.

Our first destination was the Mnajdra lower temple; our measuring tool was the Sun itself. Sunrise, we were told, was due at 6:07:45 a.m. local summer time. We were there ahead of time, straining our eyes and readying our cameras . . . As the minutes passed, the darkened skies to the east-northeast began to light. Our eyes were glued to the indicated aperture in the stone portal (fig. 69). The moment of Heliacal Rising,

Figure 69

when the reddish globe of the Sun appears against the background of the still dark-starry skies, was coming. And then a golden ray of the Sun burst through the portal, painting a ray of light on the marker stone, and we managed to commemorate the moment with our cameras (plate 22).

This Mnajdra structure was definitely a Solar "Temple"—but when was it built?

The members of my group were filled with pride of achievement, but I shook my head with doubt: Should the Sun's ray have struck the marker stone (see S3 in fig. 68, page 105) *after the passage of 5,689 years,* as Micaleff had calculated in 1979?

As we sat down outside the temple to eat the boxed breakfasts that the hotel provided to us, I reminded my group of what we had seen at Stonehenge. There, even though the marker stone called the Heel Stone was moved, at least once and probably twice, the line of sight has shifted off it (see fig. 59, page 95). If Mnajdra is *older* than Stonehenge by more than a thousand years, should the ancient alignment here still work? In Egypt, I said, a temple orientation to the solstice had to be changed every few centuries; so the fact that we did see the Sun's rays strike the marker stone might suggest that the temple here is much more recent than it is purported to be. With so many factors needed to arrive at the Declination angle, the slightest change in the calculations made a difference of centuries. The temple's Very Old Age, I felt, remained in doubt.

We then walked down to the nearby Hagar Qim. Situated on the island's southern coast, it offers a spectacular view of the Mediterranean Sea and of a tiny uninhabited island off the coast. It is, after Ggantija, the largest temple complex—situated like it at the water's edge, yet quite different from it. In addition to the massive natural stone boulders as at Ggantija, here many stone slabs are cut and fashioned, smoothed and shaped, with clear passages and entranceways whose large stone-posts and lintel stones create trilithons. Hagar Qim was undoubtedly built by talented stonemasons, with an artistic touch expressed in artfully shaped and decorated stones that some call "altars." It was at Hagar Qim that two of the Fat Goddess statues were found.

The temple's layout strongly suggested that the main entranceway to the cloverleaf part, with its "Holy of Holies" at the far end, was also purposely oriented to the Sun—in this case, to the southwest, which meant Winter Solstice. With some of us positioned at the strategic points and using strings that we brought with us, we tried to establish astronomical view lines. We ended up convinced that Hagar Qim too was a Sun Temple; and its *originally suggested* date—between 2400 to 2200 B.C.—made sense to us.

Our investigative tour of Malta's temples ended with what all deem the latest of them all—the one at Tarxien. Now surrounded by residential houses not far from Valletta, it has the appearance of an open-air museum, with its beautifully fashioned stonework giving an impression that the craftsmen have only recently left. The stone blocks are ashlar-like, precisely cut and angled; the wall behind the presumed Holy of Holies is perfectly semi-circular; stone blocks are decorated with reliefs and friezes dominated by the spiral motif, and are accurately done. A large statue of the Fat Goddess, of which only the bottom part remains, stands in an open courtyard, right at the main entrance, as if placed there by a museum curator. Tarxien's *archaeologically established date,*

2200/2100 B.C., made more sense to us than the exaggerated archaeoastronomical claims.

So when exactly were all these temples built? Even at the less distant dates, the feat was extraordinary; so who were the builders, and what was the purpose?

The United Nations, when it declared in the late 1980s seven of these temples as a World Heritage, considered them to have been built between 3000 and 2500 B.C. In my varied writings I have suggested that circa 2200 B.C. a Divine Architect—the god called by the Sumerians Ningishzidda, by the Egyptians Thoth, and by the Mesoamericans Quetzalcoatl—roamed the Earth and taught Man how to erect calendars in stone with which to determine the Zodiacal Age. It was done in the context of a mounting conflict between the Enki and Enlil clans, a conflict that led to the use of nuclear weapons in 2024 B.C.

It is in that, I still believe, that the explanation for Malta's Temple Mysteries will be found.

***

Before we left Malta, we had to see its other puzzling enigma—*the Ruts*.

The dictionary defines *rut* as "a narrow channel or groove in something, especially one made by wheels of a vehicle." The dictionary's definition aptly describes what we saw: parallel grooves cut into the ground. The mystery is that these parallel grooves have been ***cut into solid stone,*** and could not have been made by wheels of a vehicle—***because neither wheels nor vehicles existed in Neolithic times;*** and even if they did, no grooves could be made by passing wheels in the hard rocky ground.

The grooves that are usually referred to in Malta as "cart-ruts" were once visible in many places in Malta, but mostly in its western part and even on Gozo. But urbanization has obscured the ruts in many places, and the one place where we spent considerable time was left as an unoccupied field, fenced off from its surrounding and encroaching buildings (fig. 70)—an amazing relic from an unknown time, for there is no way to verify the date of a groove in a rocky field.

Figure 70

The ruts run mostly, but not exclusively, as a pair of parallel grooves—as indeed the parallel wheels of a cart would leave in a muddy trail (plate 23); except that, as stated above, the terrain is neither muddy nor soft in any way, but hard solid rock; oddly, where the soil is softer clay rather than hard limestone, no cart-ruts have been found. The grooves are sometimes a single pair, sometimes manifold. Their width varies—quite substantially, from about 4 inches to more than 20 inches. Their depth varies too—from mere surface markings to some 24 inches deep, and the variations appear even within the groove-run of the same rut. The distance between parallel pairs, though averaging about 55 inches, also varies—not only from pair to pair, but even in the course of the same groove pair.

If one would assume that discovering from where to where the ruts lead (or have led) would offer an answer to the ruts' enigma, one is disappointed: They sometimes run in the same direction, but as often as not veer aside, turn, crisscross each other—as in a place nicknamed "Clapham Junction" after a busy railroad hub in England (plate 24). They run up cliffs and down slopes, as if the terrain didn't matter. Were they related to the temples or somehow made by the temple builders? The ruts' directions do not lead to any temple sites. They sometimes run for a short distance and abruptly stop—or seem to run without end, in some cases all the way to the shore and underwater on the sea floor—an indication, some think, that the ruts were made before the sea level rose.

Of all the unanswered questions of Who, When, By Whom, Why, and so on, the one that seems to defy all reasoning is HOW. *No matter whether left by wheeled carts or otherwise, by Neolithic people or Bronze Age men, for this purpose or that—how on Earth were these grooves cut so deeply into solid rock?*

We left Malta without an answer.

7

THE ICEMAN OF
THE ALPS

There is one more interesting archaeological site in Malta; called
the Hypogeum, it is a maze of underground chambers, hewn
out of the rocky ground, that served as a subterranean City of
the Dead. The bones of thousands of people were found there; and I and
my group skipped the pleasure. But oh how I wished we could get hold
of a real fellow from those millennia ago, and find out more!

The wish, in a manner of speaking, was fulfilled a year later.

The ultra plump female images—the "Mother Goddess" statues
and statuettes—that were found in Malta were not unique. Called by
archaeologists (undoubtedly with tongue-in-cheek) "Venus figurines,"
they have been found elsewhere in European Neolithic sites, in fact all
the way to the eastern Mediterranean. That, and the probably correct
assumption that Malta's early settlers had come from Italy via Sicily,
aroused my curiosity to see for myself **the Iceman of the Alps.**

High in the Alps mountains of the Tyrol region, where Italy and
Austria meet, millions of people cut through the sky-high peaks by using
the Brenner Pass, a natural cleft in the otherwise impassable terrain.
They do so nowadays by car or train; but thousands of years ago a lone
traveler went that way on foot. A storm, an avalanche, or something else
caused him to lie down—never to awake.

It was on September 19, 1991, that two mountain climbers discovered the frozen body in a melting glacier, at 10,500 feet above sea level. The find was notified to the Austrian police, who assumed that it was the body of a recently lost hiker: It was an especially hot summer that year, and the melting ice had already exposed several other corpses of missing climbers. But when they took a good look at the male body, they had a shock: It was utterly mummified; it must have lain frozen in the ice for many decades.

Police forensic experts, arriving by helicopter, observed that what remained of the man's clothing seemed very odd. He wore some kind of leather or fur coat *lined with straw,* and he wore on his neck a necklace made of stones. They wondered whether the man had been buried in the ice for centuries rather than decades.

Anthropologists from the nearby University of Innsbruck were called in. They checked the man's clothing and implements. He had a sort of a backpack made of wood; a leather pouch hanging from his belt contained *fire flints* and a knife with a *stone blade.* Was he a Stone Age relic? The dead man clutched in his hand a crude axe, and one of the scientists—professor Konrad Spindler—realized that the blade was made of *bronze;* it was an axe as was used by people in the Bronze Age. Could it be that the man died forty centuries ago?

Based on the evidence before them, the Austrian scientists announced that the body was that *of a Bronze-Age man who lived 4,000 years ago!*

The news, and the photographs the police took, soon made headlines around the world (as this one in the American press, fig. 71): **A body found in an Alpine glacier was four thousand years old.**

The find was "of extraordinary scientific significance," Prof. Spindler told the press as he gave details of the steps taken to preserve the body in a low-temperature container for further examination. But what was then presented as a matter of a few weeks of examination and study turned out to be a series of discoveries over the following years—yes, *years,* not just weeks or months—with unexpected twists and turns.

***

THE NEW YORK TIMES **INTERNATIONAL** *THURSDAY, SEPTEMBER 26, 1991*

On Ice 4,000 Years, Bronze Age Man Is Found

VIENNA, Sept. 25 (Reuters) — Climbers on an Alpine glacier have found the fozen corpse of a Bronze Age man believed to have died 2,000 years before the birth of Christ.

Professor Konrad Spindler, who dat- of ancient equipment or clothing belonging to the dark-brown man, who appears to have been between 20 and 40 years old and measured 5 feet.

Scientists from Mainz University in Germany were to join the investiga-

"The man wore weatherproof clothing of leather and fur, lined with hay. The fine leather is tanned, the pieces stitched together with fine thongs.

"His equipment consisted of a sort of wooden backpack, a leather pouch hanging from his belt with a fire-flint, probably a bow, a stone necklace, a knife with a stone blade.

"But the most important discovery is an axe with a bronze head attached to a cleft shaft."

Mr. Spindler said the corpse's teeth were well worn, as would be consistent with a Bronze Age man.

The exact age of the body will be pinpointed using the carbon-14 dating technique.

Scientists, worried that their find might rot before detailed examinations can begin, were busy today preserving the remains with special chemicals, for storage in a low-temperature container.

Their tests over the next few months

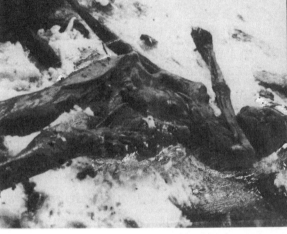

Figure 71

Once the significance of the find was realized (the body's mishandling during the first several days is a sad tale in itself), it was moved to the University of Innsbruck, Austria, where it was placed in a special room with a controlled atmosphere similar in temperature and humidity to that of his Alpine icy tomb.

Within a year, a broad portrait of the Iceman had emerged. He was in his late twenties or early thirties when he died, and was just over 5 feet tall. Presumably an outdoorsman, he was dressed for the Alpine weather. His coat was made of patches of animal fur skins, stitched together in a mosaic-like fashion with threads of animal sinew and repaired with plant fibers. Over this he wore for added warmth and protection a cape made of woven grass. On his feet he wore shoes made of leather and stuffed with hay, and on his head a furry cap.

He held in his right hand a long wooden staff pointed at the end, like a spear, and had other weapons. They included a stringless bow, and arrows in a leather quiver. The bow was made of yew—wood best suited for the purpose. The arrows, equipped with flint heads, were feathered, revealing a knowledge of aerodynamics. The quiver also contained an untreated sinew, that could be made into a bowstring; a ball of fibrous cord; a sharp thorn of a deer antler that could be used for scraping; and four antler tips. There was also the flint knife with a wooden handle, and the bronze axe earlier mentioned; except that the "bronze"—copper alloyed with tin by an elaborate process—turned out on further examination to be just plain *copper*.

The Iceman was not from the Bronze Age—he was from the earlier Copper Age. His age shifted back from 4,000 years to 4,400, then to 4,800. Radiocarbon dating of the wood and leather objects established an even earlier date: 5,300 years ago. The uniqueness of the find was amazing: ***Here was the intact body of a fully dressed and equipped European man from 3300 B.C.!***

That was more than half a millennium *after* the start of the Sumerian civilization, but a time that *predated* the start of pharaonic civilization in Egypt by two centuries. In the context of the study of the rise and spread of human civilizations, it was a find that aroused my curiosity; it was included as one objective of an Earth Chronicles Expedition after the one to Malta.

The Expedition, however, was not to Austria but to Italy . . .

To which country the unique find belonged was an issue that had its roots in the events of the discovery's first week. It is a tale that makes one wonder about the whole subject of the treatment of OOPs and the fate of other significant finds.

The couple who had stumbled upon the corpse-in-the-ice, Mr. Helmut Simon and his wife, were German tourists staying in a nearby Alpine hamlet. They hurried back to report the find, and the owner—uncertain of jurisdiction—called the police on both sides of the border. An Austrian policeman showed up the next day; the Italians never did. He tried to free the frozen body by using a jackhammer, but gave up and left. Over the weekend that followed, curiosity seekers flocked to the site, doing their best to break the ice and pluck pieces off the body and its garments. On Monday a team of police investigators arrived from Austria. Using pickaxes, they managed to free the corpse and took it to Innsbruck, where it was deposited in a local morgue. Lying unprotected, the body was shown to local reporters. It was only then that Dr. Spindler, director of the Innsbruck Institute of Prehistory, arrived at the morgue (the report that he flew to the discovery site by helicopter, seems to be a later glorified version; but it was he who had realized the uniqueness of the find).

The exposed corpse, by then almost a week out of its protective ice tomb, was beginning to show a fungal infection on its skin. Spindler's team treated the body with fungicides, wrapped it in plastics, covered it with chipped ice, and moved it to a cooled room at the university. It was thus that the Iceman was saved from rotting disintegration.

It was then that the international media, alerted by Dr. Spindler's statements that an intact body of Bronze Age man had been discovered, became immensely curious; and it was only then that the Italians awoke to the scientific and touristic potentialities of the find. They demanded a determination on which side of the Italian-Austrian border the body was actually found. When a joint survey team decided that the site was 100 yards from the border—*on the Italian side*—the Italians demanded the immediate transfer of the corpse to Italy. The Austrians said, in effect, Finders Keepers.

The compromise that was worked out allowed the Austrians to keep the Iceman—named by them Oetzi after the glacier's name—and conduct tests for three years; then he was to be handed over to the Italian authorities of South Tyrol. In fact, the transfer occurred only in 1998, when the Italians were ready to keep the body and its accoutrements in a former bank building converted to a specially equipped museum—the Archaeological Museum of South Tyrol in Bolzano, the regional capital.

It was there that I and my Earth Chronicles Expeditions group went in March 2000.

***

We left rainy Milan in the morning, and arrived in dry and chilly Bolzano, by train, in the afternoon. The rooms in our hotel (Hotel Alpi) had small balconies, enabling one to take in the Alpine view—towering mountains that seemed to compete with each other for altitude. The Museum required groups to come in by advance appointment only, and ours was for 10 a.m. the next morning.

We arrived somewhat ahead of time, and were made to wait until the doors opened. But the English-language "Record Guides" (electronic gadgets that speak into your ears explanations near each display), that were also reserved in advance, were there for us; and we were free to roam the Museum during our allotted time.

The principal "attraction" in the Museum is, of course, the mummified corpse of the Iceman. It is kept in a special sealed room, where the temperature is always −6° Celsius and the humidity is also controlled. A window is provided, through which visitors can view the body. The Iceman, with his dried-out skin now dark brown, lies in grotesque contortion, holding his wooden staff with both hands (plate 25). Did he stumble and fall like that, or was he defending himself when he froze to death?

Standing there gazing at the oldest discovered intact human body, one is seized with those and other questions, both practical and philosophical; but there is not much time given there for that, for the line of curious visitors behind you presses forward and does not let you linger at the viewing window.

Elsewhere in the Museum, video screens tell the Iceman's story, and the physical objects found with the corpse are on display. The garments he wore are laid out in the order in which he would have put them on; fig. 72 is the Museum's idea how he had looked fully clothed. His weapons and tools are also on view. Captions identify each object, and the "Record Guides" provide explanations as one stops at each display.

The visitor is unavoidably impressed by the quality and practicality —some say "sophistication"—of the physical objects from a time that

Figure 72

has been usually considered a primitive backward "Stone Age." The garments were made, and worn, to provide maximum warmth. The shoes
were shaped and fitted for walking in snow (fig. 73a). The bow was
made of Yew wood that is the best for longbows; the arrows were "feathered"; the leather pouch, that hung from his garment, contained herbal
remains that suggested it was a medicinal kit; and so on and on. True
to the Museum's announced purpose, the exhibits extend beyond the
Iceman and deal with the area in general—its climate, its people, and
their cultures in antiquity, thus putting the Iceman in the context of
his environment and his time—leaving no doubt that his time was the
Neolithic, the final phase of the Stone Age.

Before leaving, I said Hello to the Museum's director, Dr. Angelika
Fleckinger, with whom I had corresponded ahead of the visit. It would
be interesting, I suggested to her, to also have a comparative display, or at
least a panel, showing the state of civilization elsewhere—Mesopotamia,

Near East, Egypt, the Mediterranean basin—at the Iceman's time. This, I admitted to her, was my main interest: How did the Iceman's culture and technology compare to Sumerians or Egyptians of 3300 B.C. Typical of the need for specialization in an archaeological or anthropological segment to attain academic job advancement, she was an obvious expert on Stone Age Europe yet hardly familiar with Near Eastern archaeology; but she agreed that a "World Culture Map" might be a worthwhile future addition to the displays. If one was ever put up, I don't really know.

***

No one leaves the Museum without taking one more final look at the Iceman, and no one can avoid wondering: What was he doing so high up in the Alps? Presumably, he lived in one of the villages in the valley at the foothills of the mountains; so why did he go where he was found? Who really was he?

The questions have preoccupied the legion of scientists and researchers that have examined the find in every conceivable manner in the ensuing years. The series of tests, including X-rays and CAT-scans, began in Innsbruck, with experts and scientists from Vienna, from Germany, and from Switzerland called in during the very first weeks; the list then expanded to scientists and experts from Italy, and then from Britain, the U.S.A., Australia, and other parts of the world.

Over the years, the Iceman, his body, his skin, his innards, his clothing, his tools, his weapons—he and everything about him, on him, and with him have been examined in any conceivable manner of advanced technology. Varied DNA tests were conducted; Oetzi's stomach was pumped for his undigested last meal; the bacterial contents of his guts were studied; his colon was examined for fecal remains (they contained parasitic worms). His bones were tested (he suffered from arthritis). His teeth's enamel was examined for its strontium-to-lead proportions (to reveal his diet and climate conditions). The straw mantle, that he wore over the skins coat, was tested not only for age and provenance, but was also studied for the method of its knotting (fig. 73b). The metal of his axe was scanned and analyzed; blood on his arrowheads was tested. The

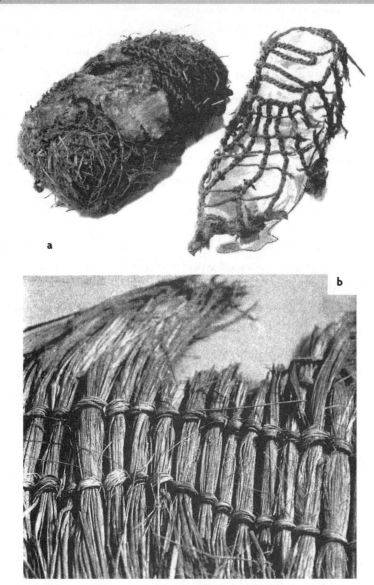

a

b

Figure 73

results revealed that the chance find was a veritable time capsule, providing rich information about the man and his humanfolk in that part of the world 5,300 years ago. The resulting conclusions and theories were also varied, diverse, and even contradictory.

His age, originally assumed to have been between 25 to 35, was upped—by some, to at least 45; he was about 5'5" tall, weighing about 65 kg (135 lbs). His skeleton and DNA were akin to those who have been living in the area to this day. The early notion that he was a shepherd was discarded after DNA tests of blood on his knife and arrowheads indicated that the blood came from other persons as well. New X-ray scans revealed an arrowhead lodged in his left shoulder; so it is now presumed that he was involved in a fight, that a comrade was with him when he lay down or fell. Tattoo marks—lines and dots—were found on his skin; did they signify a rank, social status, or (as some suggest) a religious aspect?

The latter suggestion has been reinforced by what some consider to be the most puzzling object in the "backpack": A small disc of polished stone, pierced in its center, through which it was attached to a tassel of strings. Was this a piece of jewelry—or some kind of talisman, something to ward off an "evil eye," and thus a glimpse of a primitive religion?

In the valleys at the foothills of the Alps, where the Iceman is now presumed to have lived until his mountain escapade, only mute stone tools were found from his time; there was no Cave Art, no petroglyphs, not even Fat Ladies . . . And so, all assumptions beyond the discovered physical objects are pure speculation.

***

We left Bolzano and its Iceman with several lingering questions. Why, for example, did the Sumerians at that time write on clay tablets, have high-rise temples, process metals in kilns, ferment barley to make beer, wear woven colored garments—while the Iceman needed flints to make fire? Everything about him—his clothing, his tools, his weapons—indicated high intelligence and the ability to utilize to the maximum all that was available; but what we call "technology" was way backward compared to the Sumerians of the same time. So what accounts for the difference?

To me it was a question no different from that asked in my very first book, *The 12th Planet:* Why did the Aborigines in Australia remain Aborigines to the day of their discovery in modern times? "All that we

know we were taught by the Anunnaki," a Sumerian inscription stated; the intervention of the Anunnaki "gods" was again the only plausible answer; it was they, as the ancient texts repeatedly asserted, who gave mankind its first three civilizations (Mesopotamia, Egypt, Indus Valley). Where they didn't, Man wore straw shoes in the Alps and straw skirts in Bushman Africa.

Another question concerns the issue of physical evidence of who was here and who knew what in prehistoric time: Would this unique find ever become available to scientific study were it not for Spindler's noticing of the *"bronze"* axe? Such a question similarly arose in other circumstances. Important inscribed stone tablets have been found imbedded in the walls of village abodes near ancient sites in the Near East, discovered because an archaeologist with a trained eye noticed the tablet by chance. A unique stone bowl with markings that emulate Sumerian cuneiform writing was used by a farmer in Bolivia, who had found it, as a water trough for his pigs, until someone qualified noticed the writing. What if scholars with a keen eye would not have chanced upon these objects? What if the villagers had no use for them and had just thrown them away?

We know that what has been found is a fraction of what had been—lost because of the deteriorating passage of time, natural calamities, and incessant wars. How much of what survived was found, how much of that was discarded, and how much of the remainder ended up being reported, studied—and put on display?

8

INSIGHTS TO HISTORY

The second ranking museum of Egyptian antiquities, after the one in Cairo, is neither in Egypt nor in any one of the world's great capitals. It is the *Egyptian Museum* in Turin—an industrial city in northern Italy, a city that is way out of the "Tour Italy" loop. When visitors do go to Turin, hardly any go there for its Egyptian artifacts; they go there to see the venerated *Shroud of Turin*—the purported burial cloth in which the body of Jesus was wrapped after he had died on the cross. My Italy Expedition group went to Turin to see both.

Turin is a short train ride from our assembly point, Milan—Italy's second largest city; and no sooner did we arrive in Milan than we were told the good news: The restoration of one of the world's most famous paintings was completed in time for the Holy Year 2000, and after being off limits for a long time it could be viewed again. It was thus, several years before the painting became the focus of a bestselling book phenomenon, that we were among the first to see the restored **Leonardo da Vinci's *The Last Supper*** in one of Milan's oldest churches.

As diverse and different as the objects in the three locations are, they had a great deal in common: They linked newer Faiths with older ones, B.C. with A.D., the Past with the Present. When I saw all three almost at once—in the course of just two days—**insights suddenly loomed as if a secret code was divulged, linking the Past with the Future.**

***

Turin's *Museo Egizio,* appropriately located in Accademia della Scienze Street in what is deemed the city's most characteristic domed building, has more than 30,000 artifacts from ancient Egypt, some dating back to 3500 B.C. Its establishment in 1824 was a result of Europe's growing interest in "Egyptian art" after Napoleon's expedition to Egypt in 1799. He took with him to Egypt scores of scientists, engineers, draftsmen, historians, painters, and scholars from varied fields of learning for a concerted effort to find, assemble, and record the glories of ancient Egypt. The discovered temples, monuments, statues, and other artifacts were meticulously described and pictorially depicted in the multi-volume series of prints known as the *Description de l'Egypte*—books that still serve as a foundation of Egyptology.

It so happened that the French Consul General in Cairo during the years 1803–1820, Bernardino Drovetti, was a native of the Piedmont area of northern Italy of which Turin is the regional capital. An avid collector of Egyptian artifacts, he shipped back to Turin whatever he could lay his hands on. His collection of more than 8,000 objects—grand statues, other sculptures, stelas, sarcophagi, mummies, amulets, and a treasure of inscribed papyri—formed the core of the Museum's collection and is an important part of the exhibits to this day.

The Museum boasts as a highlight of its tourist attractions the Tomb of Kha who was the chief architect of the Pharaoh Amenhotep II of the Eighteenth Dynasty. The Italian archaeologists who discovered the tomb in 1906 dismantled it with all its wall paintings and furnishings and reconstructed it, with all its contents, in the Turin museum; and one can see there the shroud-wrapped deceased, his sarcophagus, his garments, and his grooming items just as when he was entombed 3,500 years ago. Another find on exhibit is actually dated to 3500 B.C.; it is a unique piece of cloth that has on it a painting of boats and hunting scenes. There is also a reconstructed temple from Nubia. The array of statuary is grandiose. But it was a crumbling papyrus, part of the original Drovetti Collection, that was the center of my attention.

When Drovetti was shipping "Egyptian art" back to Turin, ancient Egyptian writing—hieroglyphics—was still undeciphered. It was one of Napoleon's officers who found in a village called Rosetta a stone tablet on which an edict of king Ptolemy V was inscribed in three languages— ancient Hieroglyphic, late Egyptian Demotic, and Greek; it was this *Rosetta Stone* (fig. 74, now in the British Museum) that enabled a young French linguist, Jean-Francois Champollion, to decipher Egyptian hiero- glyphics in 1822. After the Turin Museum was established a couple of years later, Champollion was invited to examine its trove of inscribed objects; it was he who was first to recognize the immense importance of the papyrus that has since become known as the *Turin King List.*

Figure 74

Students of Egyptian history—and readers of my books—are familiar with the name *Manetho*. He was an Egyptian priest in the third century B.C. who was commissioned by Ptolemy I (the first Greek ruler of Egypt after the death of Alexander the Great) to write, in Greek, a comprehensive history of Egypt. The resulting work, which listed Egypt's Pharaohs by dynasties, stated that before the human kings Egypt was ruled by demigods; and before them, seven gods—starting with the god *Ptah*—reigned over the land for 12,300 years.

In time, modern archaeologists discovered Egyptian king lists that corroborate Manetho's listings. One, from the fourteenth century B.C., is depicted on the walls of the *temple of Seti I* in Abydos (fig. 75); it shows this Nineteenth Dynasty king with his son, the future famed Ramses II, facing the inscribed names of the dynastic Pharaohs who had reigned before them. Another, known as the *Palermo Stone* because it is in the Palermo Museum on the island of Sicily, begins the listings with the gods who reigned before the demigods and the human kings. Though what is extant is a fragment of a larger stela (and even the fragment has been damaged by its use as a peasant's doorstop before its importance was realized), it is certain that the list exactly matches Manetho's from the divine beginnings through the end of the Fifth Dynasty—which dates this stone document to circa 2400 B.C. And then there is the Turin Papyrus, that also begins with the divine list—starting with the god **Ptah,** followed by the other gods, then the demigods, and then the Pharaohs. It is dated to circa 1250 B.C.

There is thus no doubt that what Manetho had written about Ptah and the other divine rulers of the Lands of the Nile was based on earlier canonical documentation in Egypt—millennia-old traditions that corroborate my assertions (see especially *The Wars of Gods and Men*) that the gods of Egypt and of Mesopotamia were the same Anunnaki: *Ptah* in Egypt was one and the same god called *Enki* by the Sumerians; his firstborn son *Marduk* in Mesopotamia was *Ra* in Egypt; his other son *Ningishzidda* was the god *Thoth* in Egypt, and so on. *Ptah was held in both civilizations to have been the one who fashioned Man through genetic engineering.* He was the one, I wrote in my books, who had suggested

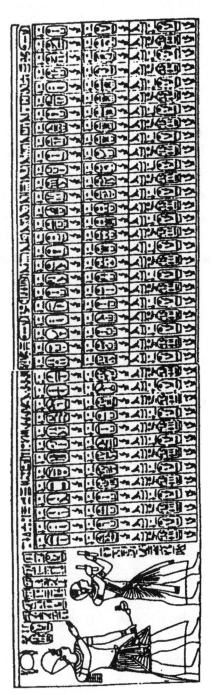

Figure 75

to the other Anunnaki leaders what the Bible states: "Let us fashion the Adam in our image and after our likeness" (Genesis 1:26).

Imagine thus my delight when we came upon a beautiful statue of a bearded Ptah—unusual in that the stone surface has a metallic glow, giving the god's staff a golden hue (plate 26)—with his hieroglyphic name prominently carved on it, looking like an entwined cord (fig. 76). It is, I explained to my group, a stylization of the more elaborate *Entwined Serpents* symbol which, in turn, represented (we now know) the *double-helix DNA*—the emblem of medicine and healing to this day. Holding in his hands the *Ankh* sign of Life, the statue depicted Ptah/Enki as the god of genetic engineering.

Egyptian finds, Mesopotamian texts and depictions, and the tales of *Genesis* in the Bible, were coming together.

"Ptah"

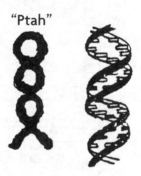

Figure 76

***

To millions around the world, Turin is known as the home of the ***Shroud of Turin***—a length of cloth, some fourteen feet long and less than four feet wide, presumed to be the shroud in which (as stated in the Gospel of Mark 15:44–46) the body of Jesus was wrapped after he was taken down from the cross and carried to a tomb hewn out of the rocks.

When the length of linen cloth is spread out, it appears to bear markings as those of a crucified body, front and back, of a man with his hands folded down. Where, according to the gospels' description of the cruci-

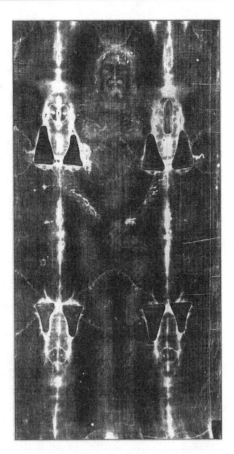

Figure 77

fixion of Jesus, his hands and feet were nailed to the cross by the Roman soldiers, bleeding wounds seem to have left their imprint on the shroud. The image is best realized when viewed as a negative, when it shows a tall bearded and moustached man, middle-aged, as in this photograph of the shroud's front image in negative (fig. 77).

The "Shroud of Turin" became associated with Turin only in 1578, when it was acquired by the Duke Emanuele Filiberto of the House of Savoy and brought to Turin. Before that it was in France, where it was kept—and exhibited on and off—since it was brought, purportedly from the island of Cyprus, circa 1350. It is first mentioned in writing in a 1389 letter from the Bishop of Troyes to the Pope, complaining that a fourteen-foot length of linen is being displayed in a church in the town of Lirey in France and "although it is not publicly stated to be the true shroud of Christ, nevertheless this is given out and noised so in private." The Bishop additionally reported to the Pope that his predecessor had ascertained that "the image is cunningly painted . . . a work of human skill and not miraculously wrought or bestowed."

The first recorded mention of the shroud was thus coupled with doubt about its authenticity—a fate that has accompanied the shroud to this day. But in spite of the Bishop's assertion that the shroud was not a relic from the time of Jesus, the shroud attracted multitudes of Believers and local nuns attributed to it miraculous healing powers. In 1578 the royal House of Savoy acquired the shroud, moved it to Turin, housed it in a special chapel, and commissioned famed painters to depict the shroud in religious-art style; one (fig. 78) even shows the shroud being repaired.

Figure 78

Until the invention of photography, the paintings served as a power-ful visual means to propagate the shroud and infer to it religious sacred-ness. The first photograph of the relic was taken in 1898, and the fact that its negative was clearer than the positive launched suggestions that the image on the shroud is itself some kind of a negative imprint miracu-lously deposited on the cloth. As both veneration and doubts contin-ued, the Church permitted in 1978 some scientific examination of the shroud; it was reported to have confirmed its authenticity. A decade later the cutting off of a postage-stamp size piece of the cloth for carbon dating was allowed; it dated it to "1260–1390 A.D." The disappointing result was duly challenged, and in 1993 a re-examination suggested that bacteria, mold, or a fire in 1532 affected the carbon dating result by some 1300 years—pushing the age of the cloth back to the time of Jesus. Other varied tests and analyses that followed kept the conclusions swinging back and forth—and the controversy continues . . .

The relic is enshrined, folded inside a silver casket, in the Chapel of the Holy Shroud of the Cathedral of San Giovanni Battista and is unrolled for display only on special occasions; the Holy Year 2000 was one of those rare times—and we went to see it during our day in Turin. Entering the dimly lit chapel and reaching the cathedral's domed part, the casket could be seen resting on an imposing marble altar; above it, the shroud itself, framed and protected by sheets of glass, could be seen fully unrolled (plate 27). The image, in faded brownish-yellow color, was exactly as we had seen it in photographs, *and it looked authentic.* But whether it really was, turned out to be doubly doubtful: First because of the ongoing controversy, and second because, to our dismay, we heard later that what we saw displayed was a replica and not yet the original—the original would be exposed only later that year . . .

So is the length of cloth two thousand years old? Is it a burial shroud? Is the image an imprint of a crucified man, or just a painting no matter how cleverly done? And if the answers are Yes, Yes, Yes—is it the burial shroud *of Jesus*? No one can say for sure. The Vatican has steadfastly nei-ther endorsed the relic's authenticity nor denied it. Pope John Paul II, who went to Turin (several months after us) as part of the Holy Year ceremonies and did get to see the original shroud, spoke of its *spiritual* meaning: An affirmation of Jesus as the Christ.

To me, the Shroud of Turin was a step on the way to the mystery of the Last Supper.

***

Before we left Milan we went to see Leonardo da Vinci's masterpiece— ***The Last Supper.***

It is a mural painted by him in 1495–1498 for his patron, the Duke Ludovico Sforza, on a wall in the convent of the Santa Maria delle Grazie church in Milan, which is now a UNESCO World Heritage site. The church was damaged during World War II in an Allied air-raid on Milan in 1943; but the mural survived undamaged—a miracle that enhanced its fame and significance. The painting has undergone several restorations, starting as early as 1726; the latest restoration, intended to remove dirt and other pollution and to stabilize the painting against flaking and deterioration, used advanced scientific methods to ascertain elements of the original painting, and is therefore deemed by some to have resulted in the most authentic version—while other experts have been unhappy with the brighter and stronger colors, preferring the older version as having a more authentic feel. This slow restoration work lasted from 1978 to 1999; it was completed in time for the Holy Year 2000—and we were, as stated above, among the first to see the restored painting that year (fig. 79).

Fifteen feet long, the painting (plate 28, after the restoration) portrays Jesus and his twelve disciples at his "last supper" before his arrest and crucifixion, as told in the New Testament. They are seated at a long table, on which food platters and round bread-cakes are seen. Jesus is in the center, flanked by his disciples in groups of three, six on each side of their Master. Each person depicted, starting with Jesus himself, is a masterful portrait painted by da Vinci to express personality, emotion, intent. The face, the gesture, the clothing, what each one holds or points to—create a lifelike and realistic scene as though it was a photograph; and indeed, from the beginning to the most recent notoriety of the

Figure 79

painting, it has been treated as though it was such—a "photograph" if not in fact, then certainly in its Church-approved interpretation of that night's events according to the New Testament.

Experts have identified the twelve disciples by their New Testament names, starting with Batholomew, James the lesser, and Andrew on Jesus' extreme right, and Matthew, Jude, and Simon on his extreme left. Judas Iscariot, who has been accused of betraying Jesus (fourth from the left) is shown wearing green and blue, the colors of betrayal according to the experts.

The photographic quality of da Vinci's masterpiece appears to have captured the group at a moment of great excitement. Interpreters of the painting have suggested that it was the moment, reported in John chapter 13, when Jesus announced to his disciples that one of them would betray him; but that happened after the meal was over and Jesus, having taken his clothes off, washed the disciples' feet. There was something else—during the meal—that agitated the group.

One could not discuss these points in front of the painting, since the group's allotted twenty minutes of viewing were up. Back at the hotel, at the last group briefing before leaving Milan, I pointed out that in two days we covered 5,000 years of history. But the discussion centered on the "Jesus exhibits"—the Shroud, the da Vinci painting. Members of the group voiced their reactions to what we had visited, what we had seen. The disciple to the right of Jesus seemed to evoke the greatest curiosity; someone recalled a book that suggested it was a female, Mary Magdalene. Others wondered what the disciples were agitated about.

As far as I am concerned, I said, it is not so much what the painting shows, but *rather what it does not show.* To understand my puzzlement, I added, one must realize that the "Last Supper" that Jesus and his disciples were having was a traditional and ritually prescribed Jewish *Seder*—the Passover-eve meal, the holiday commemorating the Israelite Exodus from Egypt.

A principal role in the Passover *Seder* meal is played by the *Prophet Elijah,* who was taken up in a whirlwind to be with God and who was to reappear, at Passover time, as the Herald of the Messiah. Custom required that a special cup, a goblet filled with wine, be set on the table for Elijah, and a hymn is sung calling upon him to appear, sip from his cup, and usher the messianic time. This custom, I said, was followed by Jesus, to whom the appearance of the Herald was vital; he held up the cup of wine and made the blessing, according to the New Testament; **but in the painting there is no cup, no goblet where Jesus sits,** I said; Why?

Is this the mystery of the Holy Grail?

Years later, as I was writing *The End of Days,* I realized that I have indeed found the answer in this painting of **The Last Supper.**

9

VATICAN ENCOUNTERS

O ne can visit Italy, the destination of the 2000 Earth Chronicles Expedition, countless times without exhausting that country's places of interest; the Vatican in Rome is just one of them. The customary Briefing Notes prepared by me for that Expedition began with a map of Italy on which I circled five destinations (fig. 80); with the exception of Bolzano and its Iceman, they all had to do—one way or another—with the Vatican, the heart and mind of the Catholic Church and its billion and a half followers around the world.

There were specific reasons for our going to each one of the marked places; but underlying it all was the curiosity stemming from persistent rumors that "The Vatican"—as a depository of covert knowledge and secret artifacts accumulated over the millennia—*knows more than it divulges about what was and what will be; that it even knows about "my" Anunnaki and their planet, Nibiru.* And to find out as much as possible about that was an added personal purpose of the trip.

Indeed, the very reason for going to Italy at that particular time was directly connected to the Vatican: To meet, and have a public dialogue, with one of its spokesmen *on the subject of Extraterrestrials.*

It has been some two or three years by then that word had reached me that a certain member of the Vatican hierarchy—a Monsignor, no

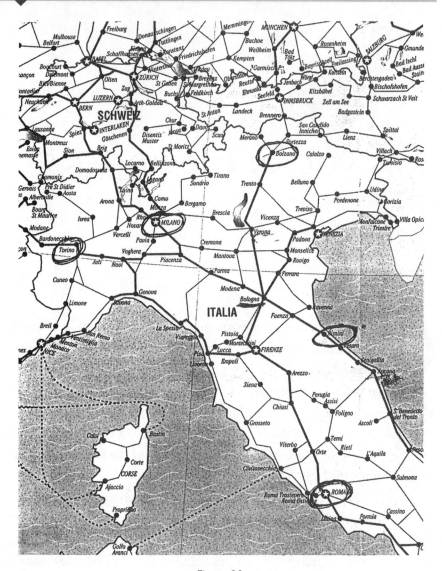

Figure 80

less—who has been speaking on the subject of UFOs and Extraterrestrials on Italian television and in press interviews, has mentioned my books.

That, the reader should be told, was not the first time that my writings were noticed by Christian clergymen. Already in 1978, two years after *The 12th Planet* was published, I shared an interview on a Christian radio program in Chicago with a Presbyterian Pastor, Rev. Jack Jennings, of the Christus Collegium in Montana, who had this to say about my book: *"The possibility that Man is not the only intelligent life in the universe and that astronauts from outer space may have been involved in Man's origins and development is supported by enough evidence to merit serious consideration."* Several years later, I found out that a Catholic priest, Father Charles Moore in California, was quoting from my books on his weekly radio program; we later appeared together on TV and he was a presenter at a Sitchin Studies Day in 1996 in Denver. Other clergymen attended and spoke up at my various seminars.

But now the clergyman who spoke out was of a different caliber . . . His name was Corrado Balducci, and he was a respected theologian high in the Vatican hierarchy, a member of the Curia of the Roman Catholic Church, a Prelate of the Congregation for the Evangelization of Peoples and the Propagation of the Faith, a member of the Vatican's Beatification Committee that approves sainthoods, the author of several books. He was actually designated by the Vatican to speak out on the UFO/Extraterrestrials subjects, I was told; and people in Italy wondered whether I had any plans to come to Italy and meet with him.

At one point it was arranged for me to speak at a conference in Sardinia which he was also due to address; but he canceled his participation at the last minute, and our meeting did not take place. Then, early in 2000, the organizers of an international conference titled *Il Mistero dell Esistenza Umana* invited me to come to Italy in March, assuring me that the Monsignor will also be there and will be ready to have a dialogue with me—a *public* dialogue.

And so it was that on Friday March 31, 2000, I and my wife and twenty of my American fans took the train in Bolzano and arrived in Rimini, a resort town on the Adriatic Sea, for the "Mystery of Human Existence" conference. The venue was a huge Centro Congressi Europeo in the adjoining town of Bellaria; I was scheduled to speak there the next day, the Monsignor on Sunday morning, and our dialogue was to take place Sunday afternoon. But by Saturday morning, Balducci was nowhere in sight . . .

I left for the conference venue certain that the Monsignor had reneged again; but when I arrived there and was led to the speakers' room, a befrocked tall Catholic priest welcomed me with open arms; he took both my hands in his, and said: I am Monsignor Corrado Balducci, and I have great esteem for your scholarship; I drove the whole night from Rome to hear you speak! It was Friendship At First Sight, commemorated by many photographs (plate 29).

As I was led to the speaker's rostrum, I was astounded by the size of the audience—there were more than a thousand people there. My talk, ably translated by my Italian editor Tuvia, included a slide presentation that added a pictorial dimension to the textual evidence from ancient times, supporting my conclusions about the planet Nibiru and the Anunnaki who had come from it to Earth and then used genetic engineering to bring about The Adam. That, I said, is the Sumerian explanation of the mystery of Humanity and its civilization; and in doing that these gods with a small "g" acted as emissaries of the Universal Creator—God with a capital "G."

"We have much to talk about," Msgr. Balducci said to me as he came forward to congratulate me on my presentation. "Shall we do it at lunch?" I suggested. We all returned to the hotel, and the restaurant set aside a table for me, my wife, and Msgr. Balducci (fig. 81); the rest of my group sat at tables surrounding us in a semicircle. Several in my group, as on an unspoken command, triggered their tape recorders: *It was not every day that a representative of the Vatican and a descendant of Abraham were about to discuss Extraterrestrials and the Creation of Man.*

Yet, in what surely was a historic first, our conclusions converged. Though different from each other in background, upbringing, religion, and methodology, we arrived at these common conclusions:

- Extraterrestrials can and do exist on other planets.
- They can be more advanced than us.
- Materially, Man could have been fashioned from a pre-existing sentient being.

Figure 81

***

In the hours-long session, Msgr. Balducci outlined the Church positions he was going to state in his talk the next day. From time to time he read from his prepared text, and then agreed to give me a copy, so that when his words are given here in quotation marks, they are actual quotes from his text or from the taped record.

It was clear that while my approach was based on the available physical evidence from antiquity, his was a purely Roman Catholic theological-philosophical one. Based on the taped recording and his prepared text, these were the positions expressed by Msgr. Balducci:

> **On UFOs:** "There must be something to it." The hundreds and thousands of eyewitness reports leave no room for denying that there is a measure of truth in them, even allowing for optical illusions, atmospheric phenomena, and so on. Such witnessing cannot be dismissed by a Catholic theologian: "Witnessing is one

way of transmitting truth, and in the case of the Christian religion we are talking about a Divine Revelation in which witnessing is crucial to the credibility of our faith."

On life on other Planets: "That life may exist on other planets is certainly possible; the Bible does not rule out that possibility. On the basis of scripture and on the basis of our knowledge of God's omnipotence, His wisdom being limitless, we must affirm that life on other planets is possible."

Moreover, this is not only possible, but also credible and even probable. "Cardinal Nicolo Cusano (1401–1464) wrote that there is not a single star in the sky about which we can rule out the existence of life, even if different from ours."

On intelligent Extraterrestrials: "When I talk about Extraterrestrials, we must think of beings who are like us—more probably, beings more advanced than us, in that their nature is an association of a material part and a spiritual part, a body and a soul, although in different proportions than human beings on Earth." Angels are beings who are purely spiritual, devoid of bodies, while we are made up of spirit and matter and [are] still at a low level."

"It is entirely credible that in the enormous distance between Angels and humans, there could be found some middle stage, that is beings with a body like ours but more elevated spiritually. If such intelligent beings really exist on other planets, only science will be able to prove. In spite of what some people think, we would be in a position to reconcile their existence with the Redemption that Christ has brought us."

These were far-reaching statements, in which I saw the basis for his being "reconciled" with my conclusions; but his comments skipped over a major point: The Creation of Man . . .

Well then, I asked Msgr. Balducci, does it mean that my presentation was no great revelation to you? We appear to agree that more advanced Extraterrestrials can exist, and I use science to evidence their coming to Earth; but then I quote the Sumerian texts that say that the *Anun-*

naki ("Those who from Heaven to Earth came") genetically improved an existing being on Earth **to create the intelligent being that the Bible calls Adam.** Do we have a conflict in that?

The Monsignor must have been ready for the challenge. My conclusion regarding your overall presentation, he said, is that more than anything else your whole approach is based on physical evidence; it concerns itself with matter, not with spirit. This is an important distinction, "because if this distinction is made, I can bring up the view of the great theologian Professor Father Marakoff, who is still alive and who is greatly respected in the Church. He formulated the hypothesis that when God created Man and put the soul into him, perhaps what is meant is not that Man was created from mud or lime, but *from something pre-existing, even from a sentient being capable of feeling and perception.* **So the idea of taking a pre-Man or hominid and creating someone who is aware of himself is something that Christianity is coming around to**. The key is the distinction between the material body and the soul granted by God."

This, I realized, was important—but it circumvented the role of the Anunnaki. Yes, I responded to the Vatican theologian, in my writings I deal with physical evidence; but already in my first book, *The 12th Planet,* the last sentence of the last paragraph raises the question: If the Extraterrestrials, the Anunnaki, "created" us, who created them on their planet? From that my own thinking and the content of my subsequent books evolved toward the spiritual or "divine" aspects. I explained in the books that the Anunnaki were just emissaries, which is what the Hebrew word *Malachim,* translated "Angels," means. They thought that it was their decision to come here for selfish reasons and to fashion us because they needed workers, but in truth they only carried out the plans of an Almighty God.

If such Extraterrestrials were so involved, Msgr. Balducci said, even by your own interpretation they had to do with Man's physics, body and rationality; but God alone had to do with the soul!

Well, I said, my second book which deals with Man's aspirations to ascend the heavens is titled *The Stairway to Heaven;* it seems to me that you and I are ascending the same stairway to heaven, though by different steps: I pursue the physical evidence, you pursue the soul! "We can agree on such a division of labor," the Mosignor answered.

It was late in the afternoon; we agreed to continue next day, in front of the public audience. But next day the program turned chaotic, with speakers holding forth well beyond their allotted time, angry exchanges, and protests from the audience. The programmed dialogue was lost in the commotion.

When the Msgr. and I said good-bye, we parted as friends, promising to stay in touch and continue. For a while we did, even considering the possibility of a joint book; but then the contacts petered out. As far as I know, Msgr. Balducci continued to speak out and state the Vatican's position on Extraterrestrials: **They can and do exist.**

***

That Msgr. Balducci's analytical approach—of building his conclusions upon a foundation of earlier Church theological opinions—was a traditional Catholic methodology, became evident as my group arrived in Rome and we went to the Vatican—with the group to the various publicly accessible parts, and I additionally to the hallowed Vatican Library for a private meeting with its director.

Rome has always evoked in me a feeling that there is more to the city's roots that links it to the ancient lands—more, *and earlier,* than the known chapters of the Punic Wars with the Phoenicians of Carthage (second century B.C.), the conquest of the Near East and Egypt in the first century B.C., and the subsequent fateful events in Judea and Jerusalem that lie at the core of Christianity.

Names, numbers, and tales associated with Rome and Roman history nagged at my sense of historical connections: According to the Roman historian Virgil, Rome's first settlers were refugees from *Troy*—i.e., people from Asia Minor. *Twelve* of their kings ruled there for three centuries. The last of those kings, afraid of the twins Romulus and Remos (sons born to a daughter of a murdered king) ordered the infants thrown into the river to die—a tale that echoes the Sumerian story of *Sargon of Akkad* and the biblical story of Pharaoh and *Moses*. When they grew up (suckled by a she-wolf), Romulus killed Remos (the tale of *Cain and Abel*) and, guided by a divine omen, ploughed a furrow around the Palatine Hill and founded there the settlement that was named after him, "Rome"—a city built on *seven* hills. Both seven and twelve were key numbers in Sumer and in the Bible.

And then there is the Vatican itself, with its links to *the twelve* Apostles; with St. Peter's basilica built, like the earlier temple of Solomon in Jerusalem, as an equinoctial temple facing precisely east (fig. 82a, b); with an *Egyptian* obelisk in the center of St. Peter's round plaza which is marked off to indicate the *twelve* houses of the *Zodiac*. The links to the ancient past, on the other side of the Mediterranean Sea, are all over the place.

Historians speak of the societal organization in the ancient Near East as that of "city-states." Nowadays, the Vatican is that kind of entity: It is a state within a state (Italy) and a city within a city (Rome), surrounded

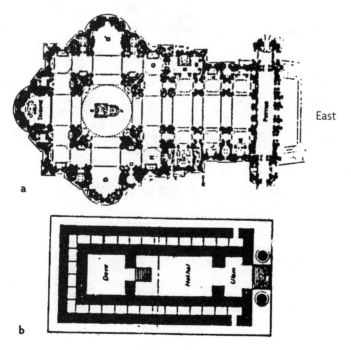

East

Figure 82

by its own defensive wall (fig. 83), a status arranged by a treaty signed in 1929. People are unaware of that as the tour buses unload them in St. Peter's Plaza and they flock, unhindered, to St. Peter's basilica. But come to the entrance that leads to the Apostolic Palace (as I and my wife did to reach the Library), and you go through Passport Control exactly as when you reach an international border . . .

***

The Vatican Museums, public entry to which is from a side street, consist of a series of galleries housed in various sections of buildings that also serve as papal palaces—residences and administrative offices; fig. 84 lists the main collections and shows their locations.

The sheer size, variety, and profusion of exhibits in the museums

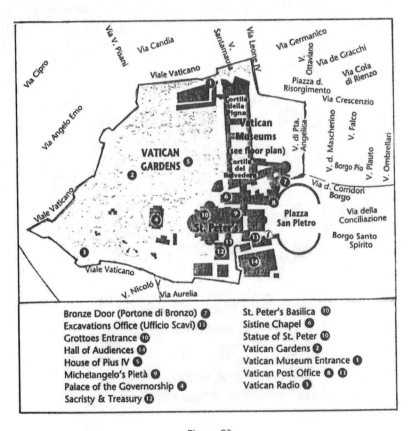

Bronze Door (Portone di Bronzo) ⑦	St. Peter's Basilica ⑩
Excavations Office (Ufficio Scavi) ⑪	Sistine Chapel ⑥
Grottoes Entrance ⑩	Statue of St. Peter ⑩
Hall of Audiences ⑭	Vatican Gardens ②
House of Pius IV ⑤	Vatican Museum Entrance ①
Michelangelo's Pietà ⑨	Vatican Post Office ⑧ ⑬
Palace of the Governorship ④	Vatican Radio ③
Sacristy & Treasury ⑫	

Figure 83

The Vatican Museums

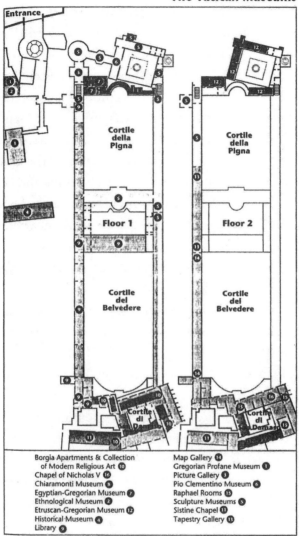

Borgia Apartments & Collection
of Modern Religious Art ⑩
Chapel of Nicholas V ⑯
Chiaramonti Museum ⑧
Egyptian-Gregorian Museum ⑦
Ethnological Museum ②
Etruscan-Gregorian Museum ⑫
Historical Museum ④
Library ⑨

Map Gallery ⑭
Gregorian Profane Museum ①
Picture Gallery ③
Pio Clementino Museum ⑥
Raphael Rooms ⑮
Sculpture Museums ⑤
Sistine Chapel ⑪
Tapestry Gallery ⑬

Figure 84

require at least several days to be fully seen, appreciated, and understood. We had to skip a good deal, and only went to the *Egyptian Museum* which also includes some Mesopotamian objects, spent time in the *Etruscan Museum*—the mysterious pre-Roman Italians whose writing emulates the ancient Hebrew alphabet, and—passing through the *Pinacoteca,* a gallery of paintings and tapestries from the eleventh to the nineteenth centuries—made our way to the unique *Sistine Chapel.*

The Sistine Chapel, built between 1475 and 1481 and part of the Apostolic Palace, originally served as the papal prayer chapel and is where the Sacred College of Cardinals are sequestered to deliberate and elect a new Pope. From the very beginning, it was built and decorated to evoke Jerusalem and the Old Testament. Rectangular in shape, the chapel measures 40.93 meters long and 13.41 meters wide (about 135 by 44 feet)—duplicating, it has been claimed, the exact measurements of Solomon's Temple in Jerusalem. The walls and ceiling of the chapel are covered with religious-theme frescoes painted by the leading late fifteenth and early sixteenth centuries Renaissance painters. While the wall frescoes are devoted to scenes from the life of Moses and Jesus, most famous are those on the arched ceiling by *Michelangelo* that depict scenes from the biblical book of *Genesis.*

We were in luck, for this famous chapel was closed for a long time for the renovation of its world-renowned frescoes, and was reopened to public entry by Pope John Paul II in time for the Millennium Year 2000, just months before our Expedition to Italy. We could thus go in, and view the famed paintings in their restored original colors.

The most famous, most copied, and most insightful frescoes are Michelangelo's scenes from *Genesis*—including the majestic *Creation of Adam* (plate 30). Painted by him so as to be located precisely above the altar, *it depicts the Creator—God—in a wholly anthropomorphic shape,* outstretching his right hand in order to impart *to the already existing Earthling* (which is what *"Adam"* literally means in Hebrew) the divine element that differentiates *Homo sapiens* from other creatures (including earlier hominids).

This is a most profound understanding of the tale in *Genesis* of the Creation of Man by the *Elohim*—a term usually translated "God" but which is most definitely *plural*—who decided to fashion the Adam "in our image and after our likeness" (as *Genesis* 1:26 states). Amazingly, **it is an understanding of the biblical tale that is in accord with the Sumerian creation texts about the genetic engineering by the *Anun-***

naki that advanced Man from an existing primitive hominid to the intelligent *Homo sapiens.*

In those texts, as elaborated in my books *The 12th Planet* and *Genesis Revisited,* the genetic feat was attained by Enki, assisted by the goddess Ninharsag and his son Ningishzidda, whose Sumerian name literally meant *"Lord/god of the Tree of Life."* I have therefore found it highly significant that the adjoining scene painted on the ceiling by Michelangelo, *The Expulsion from the Garden of Eden* fresco (the story of Eve and the Serpent), *depicts the Serpent as an anthropomorphic being emerging out of an entwined Tree of Knowing* (fig. 85).

These depictions are interpretations of the biblical tale that go way beyond the mere understanding that the Bible's Hebrew term *Nachash* (translated "serpent") can also mean "a Diviner" and "He who unveils secrets"—epithets of *Enki,* who in a second genetic manipulation gave the sterile hybrids Adam and Eve "Knowing"—the biblical term for the ability to procreate. His Egyptian name, *Ptah,* was unmistakenly written by a hieroglyph that depicts Entwined Serpents—the double-helix DNA as we have seen earlier in the Turin museum (see fig. 76, page 128).

All of this echoes not "Bible belt" dogma but the ancient Sumerian sources!

Unlike the paintings in the Pinacoteca, which can be shifted and

Figure 85

hung either here or there or altogether removed, these frescoes (murals painted directly on wet plaster) are permanent depictions. There is no way that the Popes of that time would have allowed depictions that do not conform to Church theology, so they represented the official tenets of the Vatican in regard to these themes. That the profound insights expressed in these frescoes reach all the way back to the *sources*—the Sumerian sources—of the Hebrew Bible is truly mind-boggling; it can also explain why Msgr. Balducci relied in his statements on a cardinal's words from the fifteenth century—the very time of the Sistine Chapel's paintings.

There are, I have found out in my Vatican Encounters, other timing "coincidences" that boggle the mind.

***

It was because of the amazing "Sumerian insights" in the Sistine Chapel (which I have visited twice before) that I asked my Italian publisher to use his personal contacts to get me into the Vatican Library. It was part of my effort—naive as it was—to get a glimpse, any glimpse possible, of what has been persistently rumored to have been vast secret treasures in the Vatican—not just treasures in the gold-silver-jewelry sense, but a wealth of artifacts and documents of archaeological, historical, and even pre-historical value.

For two millennia, Roman generals and emperors, Church emissaries, powerful patrons paying homage, and generations of pilgrims have brought to the Vatican precious works of art, rare artifacts, and book and manuscript collections from all over the world—including the ancient lands. Some were gifts, some were booty—as often as not taken from the sacred sites and temples of other peoples, such as the sacred candelabra and other ritual objects from the Temple in Jerusalem (which are depicted on the Arch of Titus, fig. 86).

Where are all these relics and priceless documents? While some are on view in the Vatican's public and private areas, where are the rest of them? The Vatican Library and Museums are part of the answer; but the bulk have ended up stored in the cellars and underground chambers and

Figure 86

corridors below the Vatican's buildings; and some of those objects and documents—so the rumors persistently go—attest the most explosive secrets . . .

Could they include secrets concerning the Extraterrestrials of whom Msgr. Balducci—and the earlier authorities he had quoted—have spoken, and the Anunnaki and their planet of whom I have written?

The Vatican Apostolic Library was established in 1448 by Pope Nicholas V when he combined earlier papal collections of Greek, Latin, and Hebrew codices with his own collection of manuscripts, including old ones from the Church library in the rival Constantinople; it was a reach backward to some of the most ancient sources of religion and beliefs . . . In time, other collections were added by varied means, and nowadays the Library holds some 80,000 manuscripts (handwritten books) and over a million printed books, in addition to hundreds of papyri and parchment scrolls.

The Library is housed in a wing of the group of buildings that also house the Vatican Museums and the Sistine Chapel, but is reached from inside the Vatican (after Passport Control). My meeting there was with Dr. Ambrogio Piazzoni, a lay Director of the institution. He invited me and my wife to his office, and gave us a general explanation of the library and how it functions. You come highly recommended, he said, so we will gladly issue to you a Research Permit to come and work here anytime you wish.

I thanked him and asked to see some of the stuff they keep, and he led me to see the stacks, with their rows of shelves laden with books and documents; there were also closed boxes piled up. How old are the oldest you have? I asked. Fourth century or so, he answered. A.D.? I asked to make it clear; Yes, of course, he said. That is from the official beginning of Roman Christianity, I said—the Emperor Constantine, the Council of Nicaea; but I heard that you also have gospels and manuscripts from the beginning of Christianity? Ah, Yes, he answered—but they are not included in the catalogue, so they are not available to outside researchers . . .

What about Hebrew manuscripts—I understand that some were in the very first collection, I asked. Yes, he answered, we in fact collaborate with the Hebrew University in Jerusalem in studying and publishing some of them. When I was in Prague, I said, I was amazed to see books from the Middle Ages in Hebrew, some handwritten, some printed, *dealing with astronomy;* do you have any here? We'll have to check the astronomy section, he answered—we have quite a collection, including the actual oldest log records of the Vatican Observatory. Could the original Hebrew manuscripts you have be ones dealing with astronomy? I asked. He wasn't sure.

We then talked about another kind of document from antiquity— tablets, inscribed objects, depictions. As an example of my interests, I told him of the Pontifical Biblical Institute in Jerusalem and the good cooperation I received from the Jesuit priests there in my search for the artifacts from the site in Jordan connected to the prophet Elijah. When the Church is involved, where do all such finds end up? I asked. He explained that they come under the jurisdiction of the museum's people in the archaeological department. I am awaiting word when I could also meet with them, I said. Well, maybe *they* will show you some things from behind the scenes, he said with a smile.

That other meeting did not take place, and I saw no point in going again to the Vatican Library, with no chance of seeing what is deliberately kept unseen. But before leaving Rome, I went back to the Sistine Chapel and stared again at its frescoes, studying them slowly and carefully; the answer, I felt, has to be there. The walls were covered with paintings devoted to Moses and Jesus—the one who received the Ten Commandments from God, the other who Christians believe was taken to Heaven and will return; angels hovered everywhere. The ceiling told the Genesis stories of Creation, showing God in a heavenly cloud extending His hand to Adam.

There seemed to be a powerful message to the cardinals as they assemble to elect a new Pope: **God and His angels are Extraterrestrials.**

***

My conversation with the Vatican Library director reminded me that there is yet another mystery there—**the Vatican Observatory.**

That the Vatican has had an astronomical observatory is no secret; that it operates a sophisticated array of telescopes in the United States—in Tucson, Arizona—is a little-known fact, but not a secret. The fact that the observatory has been operated by Jesuits—priests of the same order that runs the archaeologically oriented Pontifical Biblical Institute in Jerusalem—has only deepened the aura of mystery and my curiosity.

The Observatory's founding is attributed to Pope Gregory XIII (1572–1585) who ordered an observation tower to be erected. Called the Tower of the Winds and located next to the Vatican Library, the still-standing tower has in its center a marble plate surrounded by the twelve signs of the Zodiac. A ceiling hole in the south lets the Sun's rays strike a meridian line on the floor; learned Jesuit priests assembled by the Pope, by charting the Sun's movements within the zodiacal circle, calculated how far the then in use Julian calendar—so called because it was introduced in Roman times by Julius Caesar—strayed from the astronomical reality. The result was the wiping of ten days off October 1582 and the introduction of a new (and current) Gregorian Calendar. Jesuit priests have been in charge of the Observatory ever since.

In 1780 the then head of the Vatican Library converted the upper part of the tower to an observatory, equipped it with the best instruments of the time, and appointed the priest Filippo Luigi Gilil, *a scientist versed in archaeology and Hebrew,* to be its director. It was he who replicated the meridian line and the zodiacal circle on a greater scale in St. Peter's Square, using the Egyptian obelisk there for a gnomon's shadow.

In the 1930s the Observatory moved to its present official site, Castel Gandolfo, the Pope's summer residence in the mountains southeast of Rome. In 1993, the Vatican erected its main telescopes on Mount Graham in Arizona, in collaboration with the University of Arizona in Tucson. It is equipped with the most sophisticated telescopic equipment. And the question that has intrigued me has been this: *Why would the Vatican have its own astronomical observatory? What need does the Church have to observe the heavens?*

An answer of sorts was provided at an international gathering of astronomers and astrophysicists at the Vatican in May 2000, held as part of the Holy Year 2000 celebrations. Welcoming the scientists in St. Peter's Basilica, Pope John Paul II offered his views on Religion and Science by stating that scientific research "is a genuine way to arrive at the source of all truth revealed to us in the Scriptures."

Press reports were more informative: "For five days 250 astrophysicists will discuss the birth and growth of "islands of stars" of which the visible universe seems to be populated; parallel to the official theme, informal discussions range from the Big Bang to *extraterrestrial civilizations."* But a leading Vatican astronomer was even more specific, as press headlines reported: "EXTRATERRESTRIALS EXIST AND THEY ARE OUR BROTHERS" (fig. 87).

This sounded very much like Msgr. Balducci speaking . . . But the headline-grabbing statement, it was reported, was made by Father José Funes, a Jesuit priest with a degree in astrophysics and one of the luminaries of the Vatican Observatory. I managed to locate him at the Observatory's address in Arizona, told him briefly that "central to my writings has been a conclusion that a planet called Nibiru by the Sumerians is a post-Plutonian planet belonging to our Solar system," and asked for information about the work and purposes of the Observatory.

Corriere della Sera | **CRONACHE** | MARTEDÌ 13 GIUGNO 2000 **19**

Il gesuita Josè Funes in un convegno dell'Università Gregoriana: «Ma le civiltà evolute sono lontane dal nostro sistema solare»

L'astrofisico del Vaticano: «Gli extraterrestri esistono e sono nostri fratelli»

ROMA — Dalle galassie alle civiltà extraterrestri il passo è breve. «In una tipica galassia, un ammasso di almeno cento miliardi di stelle, ci potrebbero essere moltitudini di pianeti gemelli della Terra, con esseri viventi come noi. Se, come io credo, essi esistono, possono essere considerati fratelli della creazione». Detta da uno scienziato, una frase del genere non stupirebbe più. Ma quando a sostenere la «pluralità dei mondi» è un gesuita con due lauree, in astrofisica e in teologia, allora si ha una misura del cambiamento della Chiesa rispetto a idee fino a qualche secolo fa considerate eretiche. Padre Josè Funes, un gesuita argentino di 36 anni, è uno dei più giovani partecipanti al convegno internazionale sui «dischi galattici», organizzato dalla Specola Vaticana nella Pontificia Università Gregoriana. Per cinque giorni, 250 astrofisici discutono come sono nate e si sono evolute queste isole stellari che popolano l'universo visibile. Ma, al di là del tema specifico del convegno, le discussioni spaziano dal Big Bang alle civiltà extraterrestri.

Dove potrebbero albergare le forme di vita evolute? «Io penso che negli altri pianeti del sistema solare esistono solo forme molto primitive, come batteri o virus. Le civiltà evolute sono lontane, per ora invisibili e irraggiungibili, come gli angeli, anche essi fratelli della creazione».

Sul fronte dei progressi della ricerca scientifica, il professor Francesco Bertola, dell'università di Padova, organizzatore del convegno e maestro di padre Funes, riferisce come stia cambiando la geografia dell'universo grazie ai risultati del telescopio spaziale. «Prima potevamo osservare solo galassie fino a un miliardo di anni luce. Ora ci possiamo spingere fino a 13 miliardi di anni luce, e studiare quindi quelle più giovani, che si sono formate poco dopo il Big Bang. Questo ci aiuterà a capire come evolvono queste fondamentali strutture dell'universo e a risolvere alcuni problemi ancora aperti come quello della materia oscura».

Franco Foresta Martin

Figure 87

Father Funes, by then on his way to Argentina for a year, was quite courteous, and we exchanged several letters; but the only information I received from him was the official printed "Annual Report 2000" of the Observatory. There was nothing in it that directly related to the bombshell statements at the international conference, in so far as actual telescopic observations were reported; but the Jesuit staff's researches pertaining to "The Evolution of Life," and to "Cosmic Destiny and Human Destiny" sounded intriguing. In a listing of public writings and lectures by the Observatory's Director, Father George V. Coyne, the focus of its efforts was made clear: ***The evolution of Intelligent Life on Earth and possibly elsewhere.***

That, coupled with Father Funes' headline declaration, suggest that Msgr. Balducci's statements stemmed from a wide-based approach in the Vatican under Pope John Paul II. But all that still left unanswered the specific question:

What exactly is the Observatory looking for on behalf of the Vatican?

10

STARGAZERS AND SKYMAPS

L ong before the Vatican had an observatory manned by Jesuit priests, the Sumerians had theirs—ziggurats manned by astronomer priests (fig. 88); and long before Copernicus (defying the Vatican!) had determined in the sixteenth century A.D. that Earth is a member of a planetary system with the Sun in its center, the Sumerians had known it to be so. They even depicted it so 4,500 years ago.

The Sumerians, whose civilization blossomed out in Mesopotamia some 6,000 years ago, are credited with a host of "firsts" that have remained essential to an advanced society. The wheel, the brick, high-rise buildings, the kiln, mathematics, astronomy, law codes, contracts (including for marriage and divorce), kingship, religion, writing—these are just a few of the more than one hundred Firsts on the list. Their cuneiform script (fig. 89) remained in use almost to the time of Jesus; and what they described in words was often depicted pictorially on *cylinder seals* (fig. 90). Cut from stones and measuring on the average about an inch in height, the engraved cylinders served as precursors of the modern roller printing press: the artist engraved in the stone the desired depiction in reverse, as a negative, which left a positive image when rolled on wet clay. They are called cylinder *seals* because that was

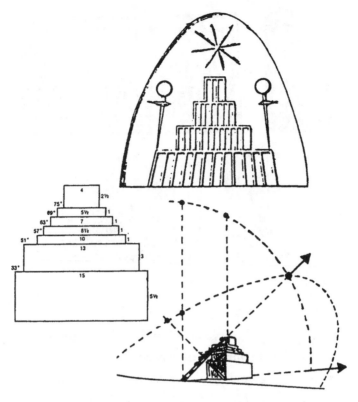

Figure 88

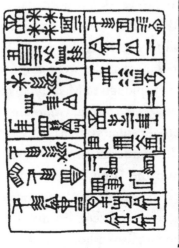

Figure 89

Figure 90

their prime purpose: To serve as a king's or VIP's personal seal, with which to stamp clay documents or clay containers.

Thousands of cylinder seals or their imprints have been found throughout the ancient Near East; every museum boasts some; scores of scholarly books and catalogues list, copy, and depict them. In the course of my researches, I have studied and examined about three thousand of them; of particular interest to me were seals adorned with celestial scenes or heavenly symbols. One day I came across a seal drawing which boggled the mind: it was of cylinder seal VA/243 in the Vorderasiatisches Museum in Berlin. Scholars said that the scene on it was "mythological"—depicting the grant of the plough to Mankind by the god of farming. ***But the celestial scene with which it was adorned*** (fig. 91) ***showed a star surrounded by planets—a solar system!***

The year was 1971. The Vorderasiatisches Museum was in what was then East Berlin, behind the "Iron Curtain." I wrote a letter to the Museum, asking for a photograph and any available information and enclosed $10 to cover costs and fees. To my surprise, I received an answer—a letter enclosing a glossy photograph to which a caption ("Sumerian cylinder seal, c. 2500 B.C.") was attached (fig. 92). The let-

Figure 91

Figure 92

ter, signed by the Museum's Director, listed a brief bibliography of published data. Research based on that left no doubt:

Some 4,500 years ago—thousands of years before the invention of the telescope—a Sumerian artist depicted our complete solar system, with its star—the Sun—in the center.

Years later, after *The 12th Planet* was published, an Internet chat group discussing the book sought the opinion of a noted astronomer regarding the VA/243 seal. "It is undoubtedly a depiction of a solar system," he posted back, "but since there is no way the Sumerians could have known that 6,000 years ago, it must be a depiction of another solar system."

When I was sent a copy of those exchanges, I wrote back on the margin: "Wow! Wow! Wow! Does he realize what he has just said?

That there was no way the Sumerians could know about our solar system, but they knew the makeup of another one—one which we have yet to discover!"

No, it was obvious from the very beginning that this was a depiction of *our* solar system. But how could the telescopeless Sumerians have known all that? The only plausible answer was: from their Anunnaki teachers. A comparison of the ancient depiction (fig. 93a) to a sketch I made of the solar system as known to us (showing the planets surrounding the Sun rather than stretched out from it fig. 93b), immediately indicated a major difference: the ancients included a sizable planet between Mars and Jupiter—where we have none. What we show in that space between Mars and Jupiter is the **Asteroid Belt**—a band of debris, *the remains of a smashed planet.*

That glaring difference bespoke the source of the ancient celestial knowledge, for the "extra" planet was Nibiru, the Home Planet of the Anunnaki.

And so, all at once, by finding seal VA/243, "pictorial" confirmation was provided for the tale in the Mesopotamian *Epic of Creation*. The text, inscribed on seven tablets, has been treated by scholars as an allegorical tale; I have treated it in *The 12th Planet* as a sophisticated cosmogony of our solar system's formation and the "celestial battle" between an invading planet ("Nibiru") which collided with and broke up the planet "Tiamat" to form out of her Earth and the "Hammered Bracelet" (the Asteroid Belt). As illustrated in my book, the sequence of events ended up with the capture of Nibiru into solar orbit (fig. 94), resulting in its return—once in about 3,600 Earth-years—to the Crossing Place, between Mars and Jupiter.

The 4,500-year-old depiction thus showed our complete solar system—Sun, Earth and the Moon, the eight other known planets (Pluto included!!!) and Nibiru, making a total of twelve (hence the first book's title).

I had visited Berlin while it was divided between West and East, at which time the tour bus kept a respectful distance from the notorious Berlin Wall at the legendary Checkpoint Charlie. But no sooner did the

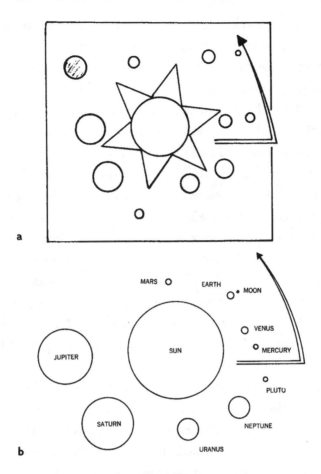

a

b

Figure 93

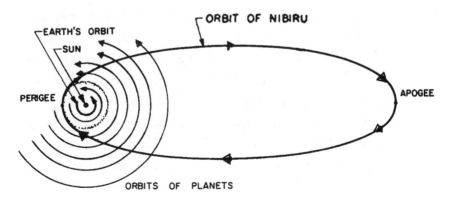

Figure 94

Wall fall than I was back, rushing in a "Western" Berlin taxi through the strange eastern part to the Museum. After a few inquiries, I was directed to the section where, inside a glass-faced display case devoted to cylinder seals, the all-important cylinder seal was on display. VA/243 was real!

In 1991 I was back in Berlin with a camera crew, filming in the Vorderasiatisches Museum video footage for a documentary based on my book *Genesis Revisited* and titled *Are We Alone?* The permit negotiated by the Swiss-based producers with the Museum allowed us to come in each day for a week two hours before the public opening, and clear out by opening time. Each day the Director—Frau Doktor Jakob-Prost—was up in arms because we didn't leave on time; each next day she acceded to our requests to film this or do that. One of those particular requests was to film a demonstration of how a cylinder seal is actually rolled on wet clay to leave the positive imprint. I suggested that we use seal VA/243 in the demonstration; but when all was set up for that, the Museum employee showed up with another seal; VA/243 was too important, they explained, to be risked.

Over the years, the Museum was visited by hundreds of my readers eager to see the seal, and its image was used and shown in countless articles and TV programs all over the world. But as far as my own "close encounter" with it was concerned, the filming in Berlin in 1991 was the last time—until an unexpected encounter in May 2000.

***

It was soon after returning home from the eventful visit to Italy during the Vatican's Holy Year 2000 that I found in the mail a large flat envelope from one of my longtime fans, Joanne N. "You'll get a kick out of this," she wrote in a note attached to several pages clipped from *Sky & Telescope,* a monthly magazine devoted to astronomy. A color photograph immediately caught my eye: it was a photograph of the original 1976 cover of my first book, *The 12th Planet* (plate 31)!

It was, as I later reported in my website, "an encounter with an old friend" and quite a surprise: What was it doing, after twenty-four years, in *Sky & Telescope*?

A closer look at the pages revealed that the photo was provided by an astronomer, E. C. Krupp, for his article "Lost Worlds" in the magazine. His subject was the misconceived predictions of planetary dooms, such as the then hullabaloo about the End of the World on May 5, 2000. Though I had absolutely nothing to do with those predictions, Dr. Krupp found the opportunity to deal—after a quarter of a century!—with "a different astronomical misconception"—my interpretation of cylinder seal VA/243 . . .

"Zecharia Sitchin's books," the article explained, are "about ancient space colonists from a lost 'twelfth planet' that once violently invaded our solar system." Lamenting (or conceding?) that "credulous readers are persuaded by Sitchin that the traditions of ancient Sumer validate this unorthodox reconstruction of solar system history," the article declared that

> Sitchin's case originates in an Akkadian cylinder seal from the third millennium B.C., a portion of which features a six-pointed star surrounded by eleven dots of varying size. Sitchin judged that the star symbolizes the Sun and the smaller elements are supposedly planets, including the lost 12th world.

The ancient depiction and my interpretation of it have embarrassed astronomers from the very beginning, because it was just not possible for the ancient peoples to have known about the post-Saturn planets, to say nothing about one more yet-unknown planet; and my explanation that the knowledge was provided by Extraterrestrials who had come to Earth made my viewpoint an even greater anathema to the scientific establishment. So now, finally—after a quarter of a century!—a noted astronomer, head of a major observatory in California, has come up with an antidote. As the magazine summed up in a sidebar, the ancient depiction of our complete solar system could be interpreted differently:

> Several other interpretations of the symbols may be entertained. They could easily represent a bright planet—such as Jupiter—in the midst of familiar stars. In fact, the arrangement around the starlike object roughly resembles the Teapot of Sagittarius.

My purported evidence for the ancients' impossible knowledge, the article stated, was no evidence at all, because *what the seal depicts is the known bright* **planet Jupiter,** *shown passing within the Teapot of the well-known* **constellation of Sagittarius;** hence, if the central "star" is not the Sun but the planet Jupiter, and the surrounding dots not planets but stars that make up the constellation of Sagittarius, there is no need for extraordinary knowledge, no Extraterrestrial teachers, no Anunnaki, no 12th planet, no Sitchin misconceptions!

Two illustrations alongside the sidebar's text illustrated the article's point (plate 32). One purported to illustrate what I claimed—not badly, but certainly not exactly the way it was depicted on the cylinder seal or in my drawings, and conveniently omitting the mysterious planet between Mars and Jupiter. The other outlined the Teapot using the cylinder seal depiction to "connect the dots," to show how it resembled Jupiter seen within Sagittarius.

***

This out-of-the-blue critique of my understanding of cylinder seal VA/243, even after a quarter of a century, was a weighty matter. *Sky & Telescope* is a prestigious journal. Dr. Krupp, then head of the Griffith Observatory in California, was a respected astronomer and the author of several books—some actually quoted in my books. His alternative interpretation of the ancient seal could not be taken lightly.

I have of course known that Sagittarius is one of the twelve zodiacal constellations; it was known to the Sumerians, was called by them PA.BIL ("The Defender") and was depicted by them as an Archer (fig. 95)—a name and a depiction retained to this day. But what the heck was its "Teapot"?

I looked it up in my books on astronomy and found out that some modern astronomers (while having afternoon tea?) decided that the central part of Sagittarius resembles a teapot: a "spout" formed by connecting the constellation's stars Al Nasi, Kaus Media, and Kaus Australis (also designated Gamma, Delta, and Epsilon); a "handle"

Figure 95

shaped by the stars designated Zeta (Ascella), Tau, Sigma (Nunki), and Phi; and a "lid" indicated by Kaus Borealis (Lambda).

I made a copy of a star map of Sagittarius, and drew on it lines to connect the above named stars as dots, in the manner that the article had used the planets in the ancient depiction to "connect the dots"; I then placed the resulting sketch next to the dot-connecting illustration in the magazine (fig. 96). Did they look alike? Yes? No? Not really? As I kept on comparing, I began to wonder: **Where is Jupiter,** supposedly passing in the center of Sagittarius, within the Teapot?

And then, as I noticed the line indicating "Ecliptic" (the plane in which the planets orbit the Sun), the realization hit me: *Jupiter is not there because Jupiter could never be there! Jupiter orbits the Sun almost precisely in the Ecliptic; it NEVER strays south to EVER have a conjunction with the center of Sagittarius;* **it can never be within the Teapot!**

I checked this astounding finding with friends who are amateur astronomers. I checked with the Planetarium of the Metropolitan Museum in New York. I checked with the prestigious Palmer Planetarium in Chicago. They confirmed my conclusion—in writing. There was no doubt: The counter solution proposed in *Sky & Telescope* was an impossibility, and my original interpretation remained standing unchallenged.

I then wrote a Letter to the Editor to the journal, politely pointing it all out. The letter was not published. But after some time, I received a

SAGITTARIUS, showing the "Teapot"

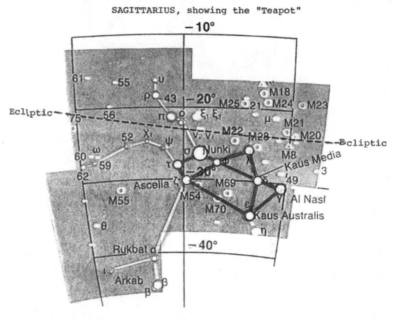

Figure 96

response—a two page letter from Dr. Krupp himself. Written on the Observatory's letterhead and dated 4 August 2000, it said:

It is a delight to hear from you. I have all your books, have read most of them, and have listened to you on the radio a couple of times. I have of course dedicated thought to the arguments you have developed. Although your handling of the data has inspired my skepticism, please let me acknowledge the courtesy and logic of your complaint about the way I evaluated your Twelfth Planet notions in my monthly column on astronomy and culture in *Sky & Telescope*.

You are correct to point out that I was hasty in offering Sagittarius as an option for the imagery on the Akkadian cylinder seal VA/243. Certainly we cannot regard the figure as an accurate map of the Teapot with Jupiter brewing inside. If you allow me Saturn, we get a little closer; but you are right—no tea caddied planet. My caption highlights Jupiter, positions it within Sagittarius, and suggests a real mapping. Your objection is sustained.

So, if he was wrong ("hasty," he called it), was I right after all? Not yet—as the letter continued:

> Of course, there are other candidates among the stars. A planet could have been in the vicinity of Leo, for example, enclosed by Regulus, gamma Leonis, zeta Leonis, epsilon Leonis, alpha Canceri, 38 Canceri, zeta Hydrae, and iota Hydra. Given the lack of precision on the cylinder seal, that set of stars works pretty well. If they be unacceptable, however, we can alternatively imagine a planet in a larger enclosure.

Should I have said "Wow! Wow! Wow!" again? Gotten angry that there was no apology? Instead, I wrote the distinguished astronomer as follows:

> It truly chagrins me that someone like you, in searching for explanations for the seal's depictions (you list some of the most improbable ones in your letter) would not even consider our solar system as a possibility. This can only stem from an absolute refusal to accept the Extraterrestrial nature of the Anunnaki. But why would someone—I am sure you are included—who would deem it possible that Man from Earth would one day travel to another planet, deem it totally unacceptable that someone from another planet might have come here?

I signed the letter "Looking forward to a dialogue with you." But as far as the others were concerned, the matter was closed.

***

In retrospect, my rhetorical question to a modern stargazer stated the issue of elitist shunning of "Extraterrestrials" in a nutshell: If we will be able someday to send our astronauts to another planet—why is it inconceivable that the reverse could—and did—happen?

In February 1971 the United States launched an unmanned spacecraft on a journey whose ultimate destination was outer space. Named *Pioneer 10,* it traveled for twenty-one months, past Mars and the

Asteroid Belt, to a precisely scheduled rendezvous with Jupiter. There the great gravitational forces of Jupiter grabbed the spacecraft and thrust it out into outer space. On the 25th anniversary of *Pioneer 10's* departure from Earth, it crossed the outermost boundary of our Sun's realm and was still coursing to destinations unknown—perhaps to tell some "Extraterrestrial" out there that the tiny planet in a certain solar system has intelligent beings who wish to say Hello.

No, this is not my fantasy. Serious scientists attached to *Pioneer 10* a plaque bearing such message (fig. 97). In sign language, it informs whomever it will encounter that it comes from the third planet in a solar system in a certain galaxy, from which intelligent beings, male and female, send greetings.

"We may never know whether, countless years from now, someone on another planet will find and understand the message drawn on the plaque attached to *Pioneer 10*," I wrote in 1976 in *The 12th Planet*. *"Likewise, one would think it futile to expect to find on Earth such a plaque in reverse . . . Yet, such extraordinary evidence does exist!"*

The evidence, I then wrote, is a plaque conveying to Earthlings infor-

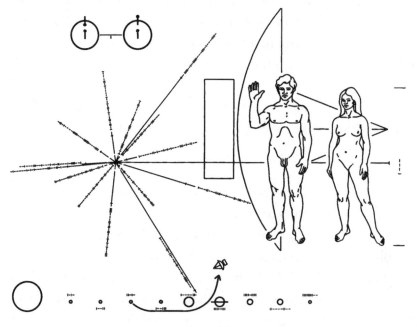

Figure 97

mation regarding the location and the route from the 12th Planet to Earth. It is a round plaque that was discovered in the ruins of the royal library of Nineveh, the capital of ancient Assyria, and is on view in the British Museum in London. Though catalogued (BM K-8538) as a clay disc, it has a gray metallic coloring to it, and where it is damaged it appears to have been damaged by fire—most unusual, for clay hardens in fire rather than softens and bends as had happened to this artifact.

The undamaged portions of the disc are covered with cuneiform signs, together with arrows, triangles, intersecting lines, and even an ellipse (a geometric shape supposedly unknown in antiquity). In 1912 L. W. King, then curator of Assyrian and Babylonian antiquities in the British Museum, made a meticulous copy of the signs, showing that the disc was precisely divided into eight segments (fig. 98).

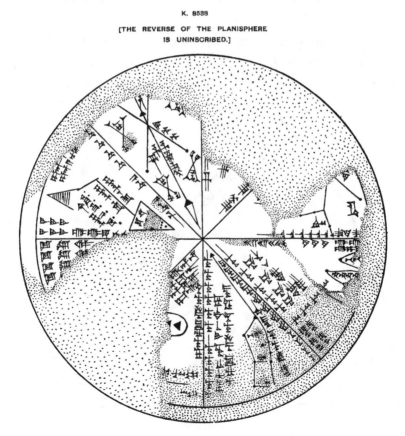

K. 8538

[THE REVERSE OF THE PLANISPHERE
IS UNINSCRIBED.]

Figure 98

The cuneiform writing clearly included the names of stars and planets, so no wonder that the unusual artifact was first discussed at sessions of the British Royal Astronomical Society, which designated it to be a 360° Planisphere—the reproduction on a flat surface of the heavens enveloping the Earth as a sphere. Yet, for reasons of its own, the Museum displays this unusual artifact in the section devoted to Writing, rather than as part of its great Mesopotamian collection. This has enabled me to first guide my groups through the Sumerian, Akkadian, Babylonian, and Assyrian displays spread over three floors and gradually introduce them to the evidence about the Anunnaki "gods," and then take them to see the separately displayed conclusive item—this "clay" disc.

"Conclusive" because what has been inscribed and described on this millennia-old document is a skymap, in which the Anunnaki showed and literally told Mankind: This is how we journey between our planet and yours.

Without repeating the extensive analysis of the planisphere given in *The 12th Planet,* suffice it to say here that the most compelling segment is the one with two connected triangular shapes. Its writing, when

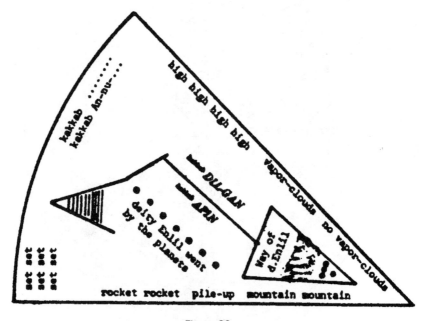

Figure 99

translated (fig. 99), consists of celestial navigation terminology with top-ographic landing directions on the segment's margins, and provides in the center ***an unmistakable route map from a mountainous planet to our segment of the solar system.*** The connecting line indicates a course correction or detour between two planets—*Kakkab DILGAN* ("Planet Jupiter") and *Kakkab APIN* ("Planet Mars"); ***the inscription where seven dots are depicted states in the clearest possible way:*** "Deity Enlil went by the planets."

That there are seven of them is no error; on the contrary, it is in conformity with the persistent referral in Mesopotamian astronomical texts to Earth as "the seventh" (and its depiction with seven dots when celestial symbols were used—fig. 100). Indeed, it could be considered as another

Figure 100

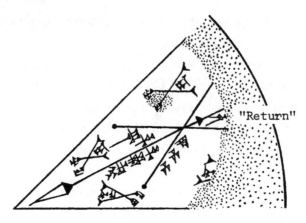

Figure 101

compelling piece of evidence for the Anunnaki and their distant planet Nibiru—for while we think of Earth as the third planet from the Sun, *someone coming into our solar system from outside would first encounter Pluto (yes, Pluto!), then Neptune and Uranus, Saturn and Jupiter; Mars would be the sixth to be encountered, and Earth the seventh!*

That, the ancient skymap states, is how the god EN.LIL ("Lord of the Command") had journeyed to come to Earth. The route correction or detour between Jupiter and Mars—where the Asteroid Belt is located—conforms to the cosmogony of the Epic of Creation and confirms the use by the Anunnaki of Mars as a Way Station.

It was not a one way celestial journey. In the eighth segment of this amazing skymap, pointing arrows are accompanied by the word RETURN (fig. 101).

And therein lies the link between the Past and the Future.

11

ANTIKYTHERA: A COMPUTER BEFORE ITS TIME

I have often told my audiences that "the Past is the Future." If a physical object could be found to illustrate that the Future was in the Past, it is without doubt the "Antikythera mechanism" in the National Archaeological Museum in Athens, Greece.

It is, one can say, the OOP to beat all museum OOPs.

The circumstances of its discovery, which help determine its age, are beyond dispute; so, beyond dispute, is its Out Of Place advanced technology. Its place of provenance (though not necessarily of origin) is more or less a good guess. But who possessed the technology that underlies the "mechanism," and what was its purpose, have remained a subject of debate and conjecture for more than a century. *It is my belief that a real breakthrough in solving the enigma will not occur until it is realized that the Antikythera Mechanism is a product of the technologies not of Man, but of the gods.*

It was just before Easter in 1900 that two sponge-divers' boats were sailing in the eastern Mediterranean, off the Greek island of Antikythera. Diving for sponges where in antiquity boats plied the Mediterranean sea route between east and west, the divers discovered on the sea floor, at a depth of 42 meters (about 140 feet), the wreck of an ancient ship. They retrieved from the wreck various artifacts, including marble and bronze statues.

The find was reported to the authorities, and the ship and its contents were subsequently examined by archaeologists and other experts, as more of the cargo's objects were retrieved. They dated the ship to some time after 200 B.C.; amphorae—clay jars that once contained wine, olive oil, and other foodstuffs—were dated to about 75 B.C. These two dates marked the "not-earlier and not-later than" dates *of the shipwreck*. By now all experts agree that the ship sank in the first century B.C.—so everything found in it had to be, in A.D. 1900, at least 2,000 years old; but the fact that some of the statues were dated with certainty to the fourth century B.C. naturally suggests that other finds in the shipwreck could also be that old, or even older.

Among the finds brought to the Museum for examination was a lump of hardened mud in which pieces of metal—presumably pieces of a statue that broke up—were embedded. It was in May 1902 that a Museum archaeologist noticed in it a rounded piece of metal that looked like a wheel. As the mud was cleaned away, the hard core of the lump was revealed to be a heavily encrusted and corroded wheeled metal object (plate 33). As its details were studied (fig. 102), and other round and teethed pieces of metal—gear wheels?—were cleaned and placed next to each other, the stunned Museum officials saw a mechanical contraption made of bronze and consisting of several circular parts including gear wheels (fig. 103). They were seeing, they realized, an amazingly complex mechanical contraption that could not possibly belong to antiquity . . .

The Antikythera Mechanism, as it came to be called, was contained in a wooden box measuring 33 by 17 centimeters (about 13 by 6.75 inches), and a mere 9 centimeters (about 3.5 inches) wide. Greek lettering was visible on the metal parts; but whether the letters added up to words, and what they meant, required a lot more delicate cleaning and matching of fragments.

Further examination and studies showed that the small box contained a precision-made mechanism consisting of numerous toothed wheels—gears—of different sizes, interlocked at different planes within

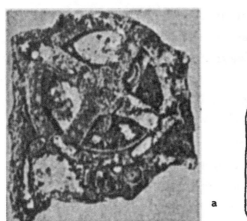

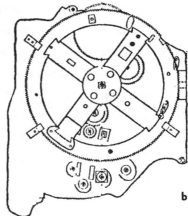

a

b

Figure 102

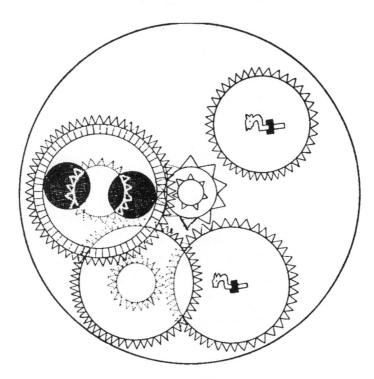

Figure 103

a circular frame (fig. 104), which in turn was held in place inside the wooden box.

So what was it, where did it come from, who made it, when, and what for? The first clues that the device's investigators followed focused on the ship itself. They concluded from the cargo that the ship was sailing from east to west, and assumed that the ship was coming from either Greek colonies in Asia Minor (today's Turkey), or from the nearby Greek islands Rhodes or Cos in the eastern Mediterranean, its destination being Italy (possibly to Rome).

Did the device originate there? It was pointed out that on the island of Rhodes there had been an academy, founded by the philosopher Posidonios, dedicated to astronomy and mechanical engineering. Was the device, then, a product of that center's engineering advancements combined with astronomy—*was it an astronomical device*? Some thought that it was some kind of planetarium, used to show the motions of celestial bodies. Others suggested that it had a practical purpose—that it was some kind of a naval instrument using the stars for navigation.

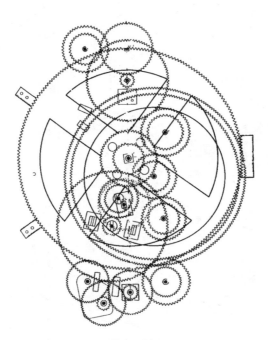

Figure 104

After several decades of investigation, the prevailing conclusion was that the mechanism was an **Astrolabe** (literally: "A taker of stars")—an instrument used to project the motions and determine the positions of the Sun, Moon, and planets—"with spherical projections and a set of rings."

And there, half a century after the discovery, the matter more or less rested.

✳✳✳

Reading about the discovery in the course of working on my first book, *The 12th Planet,* the term *astrolabe* aroused my interest. In a chapter devoted to astronomical knowledge in antiquity, I reported the sensational lecture given by the Assyriologist Theophilus G. Pinches at the Royal Asiatic Society in London, England, in that very same year— 1900—of the Antikythera discovery. His talk was about a **Mesopotamian astrolabe** from the *second millennium B.C.* It was circular and also had writing on it, in cuneiform; it was also discovered in fragments (made of clay). Pinches succeeded in putting them together to render the complete astrolabe (here with its writing translated, fig. 105).

Its special significance for *The 12th Planet* was that the Mesopotamian astrolabe listed the home planet of the Anunnaki, Nibiru, by its Babylonian name *Mul Marduk;* showed that its design and use were based on *spherical astronomy* (and thus on a spherical and not flat Earth); and confirmed the Mesopotamian familiarity with the zodiacal constellations. The latter points were part of a wider exploration in my book of the Mesopotamian origins of the astronomical knowledge for which the much later Greeks have been given credit.

Those Greek astronomers/mathematicians included Hipparchus (second century B.C.) who has been credited—wrongly—with discovering the phenomenon of Precession that lies at the core of the division of the heavens into twelve zodiacal constellations. Citing ancient cuneiform texts and pictorial evidence, I showed that the zodiacal constellations were known to the Sumerians and were named and depicted by them in the very manner we still call and depict them to this day (see fig. 56, page 93)—knowledge that takes us back to the *fourth millennium B.C.*

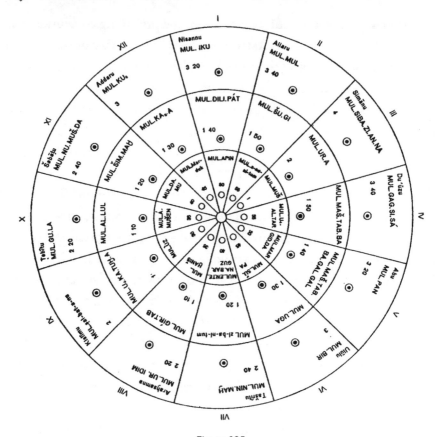

Figure 105

The better-known Babylonian astronomical texts, from the second millennium B.C., and Assyrian ones from the first millennium B.C.—which are sometimes acknowledged as the source of the Greek astronomical knowledge—were all based on the earlier Sumerian foundations.

The interesting fact in that chain of knowledge-connections is that both Hipparchus and Eudoxus lived in Asia Minor, in Greek settlements that formed a geographical and cultural link to the Mesopotamian knowledge; the island of Rhodes, the purported origin of the wrecked ship's cargo, lies just off that Greek-settled coast of Asia Minor; and both Greek savants—it is now certain—drew their knowledge from Mesopotamia's Babylon and its precursor, Sumer.

I therefore wondered whether the similarities to the "Pinches" Mesopotamian astrolabe were a clue to the true origin of the Antikythera "astrolabe"—if not its physical origin, then of the knowledge required for its fashioning. Much more was needed to be found out—especially the decipherment of the inscriptions on it—for unlocking the device's secrets. So I completed the manuscript of *The 12th Planet* without referring to the Antikythera mechanism, but planned to go and see the device for myself soon after the book was published.

The very next year, 1977, I went to visit Greece with my wife. My particular interest, I must admit, was Delphi, its famed oracle and its "Whispering Stone," the Omphalos, for reasons explained in my follow-up book, *The Stairway to Heaven*. But I of course went several times to the archaeological museum in Athens. The mechanism was on display in a back room of the Museum devoted to "Bronzes," and its explanatory caption was quite modest:

No. 15087.
Mechanism used in astronomy (astrolabus?).
Found in 1900 in the Sea of Antikythera.
System of geared discs and long Greek
inscriptions of 2nd century B.C.

There wasn't much information there, nor an impetus for further research . . .

But still curious, I wrote to the Museum, asking for a fuller story and for the latest on the deciphering attempts. Surprisingly, I did get a response from the Director, B. Philippaki, that said:

In reply to your letter of 17.10.1978, we inform you the following:

The mechanism inv.no.X-15087 was found in the sea of Antikythera island by sponge divers in 1900. It was part of the cargo of a shipwreck which occurred in the first cent. B.C. The mechanism is considered to be a calendrical Sun and Moon computing machine dated, after the latest evidence, to ca. 80 B.C.

For technical details of the mechanism and for its inscription you should consult the monograph "Gears from the Greeks, The Antikythera Mechanism" by D. De Solla Price (Science History Publications, 1975).

An older article on the subject has been published in "Scientific American," June 1959.

The letter from Athens reached me too late to follow its suggestions in time for *The Stairway to Heaven*. **But it did open up a Pandora's box of research, wonderment, and in time totally unexpected insights.**

***

Dr. Derek de Solla Price, it turned out, became interested in the mechanism already in 1951, helping to identify the mechanism's 30 gears and some 80 other different parts. In 1959, in an article in *Scientific American,* he suggested that the mechanism was a device for calculating the motions of the planets in relation to star constellations and that *it operated as a mechanical computer.* Enthused by such technological prowess by the ancient Greeks, he gave them credit for devising a mechanism that was the forerunner, not by centuries but by much more than a millennium, of medieval astronomical clocks.

Joining Greek experts, he spent another two decades studying the device during its careful cleaning and the evaluation of its diverse pieces. As technology advanced, X-rays were used to ascertain what was inside the crushed-together mechanism, and epigraphers made progress in reading the inscriptions. By then a Professor of History of Science at Yale University, de Solla Price offered his new findings and conclusions in a 1976 book with an intriguing title and subtitle:

GEARS FROM THE GREEKS
The Antikythera Mechanism
A Calendar Computer from ca. 80 B.C.

Following the suggestion from Athens, I managed to obtain the book. The cover alone (fig. 106) was highly intriguing; the contents mind-boggling. The "mechanism," to put it mildly, was a first-class OOP: The professor's findings were that the Antikythera Mechanism *"is the oldest and most complex surviving scientific instrument of antiquity—a computer from the first century B.C."*

Professor de Solla Price concluded that the mechanism's remains consisted of four major parts. It was housed in a wooden box that could be opened from front and back; the wood, however, disintegrated

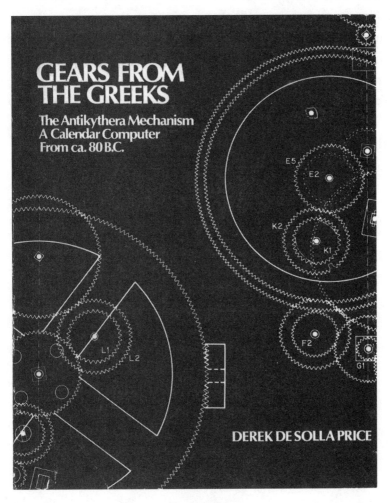

Figure 106

quickly after the object was taken out of the water in which it had been immersed for two thousand years. The most astounding aspect was the gears; he counted and identified 28 gears of varying sizes, and illustrated how they were assembled in "layers" in two groups, a front group and a back group (fig. 107), thinly arranged and "sandwiched" against each other inside the small and narrow box. He also drew a schematic plan of all the gears, showing how the teeth of one meshed with those of others, so that when the main two gears (one in front, one in the back, inside the box) rotated—probably moved by a hand crank—*all the other wheels were put into motion* (as partly depicted on the cover).

There were at least ten different kinds of components in the mechanism, each consisting of sub-parts—attachments, levers, axles, and so on. It is impossible to convey the scope of the mechanism's ingenuity and complexity without following the analysis in page after page of the book. An idea could be given, perhaps, simply by quoting some words and terminology from the book: "Structure of the dial work," "concentric pair of dials," "outer perimeter of the main drive," "central plate surrounded by annuli," "four complete rings," "a special bridge with

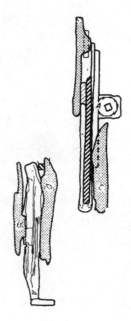

Figure 107

straddles," "a strip riveted to the central plate," "dial pointer," "engraved and inscribed fixed limb," "graduations across the annuli," "dial plate overhangs," "connecting channel-place support," "a series of tiny holes," "equilateral teeth," "rim connected to a circular hub with four spokes," "gear-train system," "planetary markers," and so on and on.

All these diverse components of the mechanism were made from a special bronze, formed into a single flat metal sheet from which all the parts were precisely cut out. Bronze is an alloy of copper with tin, a mixture that gives the soft copper great strength and rigidity. Objects made of bronze are, as a rule, the result of casting in a mold, because the alloy is not malleable. ***How*** then was a thin flat sheet—*of a thickness of less than 6 millimeters (0.24 inches!)*—manufactured, ***how*** could the parts be cut out of it with great precision, and ***how*** could the gear teeth be cut to provide the exact number of teeth around the given circumference of each (and different) gear? An astounding level of geometry and mathematics was required just for that.

The gear teeth (as later studies showed) were cut with astounding accuracy (fig. 108) at a precise and uniform angle of 60° that assured an ideal fit between gear wheels—a precise and perfect fit that allowed them to rotate each other without either slippage or getting stuck. Another mind-boggling aspect of the tight inner assemblage is the fact that the separations between the various gear levels average a minuscule gap of

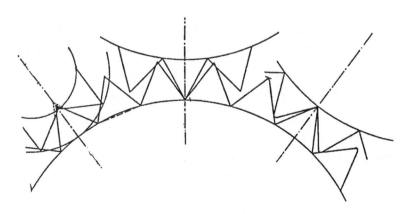

Figure 108

1.35 millimeters (0.05 inches)—a fantastic technological achievement at any time! This is almost what **Nanotechnology,** a miniaturization of mechanical components to microscopic size, is expected to achieve for us in the *future!*

How was that achieved, and by whom?

Still, what seems to have impressed the History of Science professor most was the fact that the gear wheels were of varied sizes, each with a different number of teeth, which made the whole system one of *"differential gearing"*—meaning that gears of different sizes meshed to rotate at different speeds—the smaller gears rotated more times (and thus faster) than the larger gears with which their teeth meshed (and vice versa). The different sizes meant a different number of gear "teeth"; and those differences in the number of gear teeth were not haphazard, but carefully designed to attain the overall precision of the mechanism.

"The differential gear does not appear again until it occurs in a complicated global clock made by Eberhart Baldewin at the court of Landgraf Wilhelm IV at Kassel in 1575," Prof. Price wrote. **The Antikythera device thus remained a unique forerunner of the Future from the Past for at least 1,650 years.**

***

What was the purpose of such a fantastic mechanism? The clues stemmed from three sources: The gearing, the gradational marks, and the writing.

Where the number of teeth in the various gears could be determined, it suggested to Prof. Price that the mechanism was concerned with *lunar phenomena during various solar periods.* The differential ratios indicated to him the Metonic Cycle of the Moon (by which cycle of so many Moon-months catches up with a solar-year cycle once in 19 years). The numbers also suggested a relationship with the periodic *eclipses of the Moon* during such a cycle. That some of the Greek writing spelled out the names of months strengthened his conclusions regarding the Moon/Sun aspects of the mechanism.

But the gradational marks on the circumference of the larger wheels seemed to divide the grand cycle into twelve sections each of 30°—30 *degrees,* not 30 days—and the writing thereon indicated that the division was not into months but into twelve *zodiacal* sections. Indeed, the names of zodiacal constellations, such as Libra, Virgo, Gemini, Taurus, etc., are inscribed on the circumference (indicating, I must point out, a progression as in the Sumerian manner—see fig. 55, page 92). Some of the longer inscriptions, which include references to **equinoxes and solstices,** clearly record **zodiacal phenomena.** All that suggests functions that somehow relate the cycles of the Moon, and not just the Sun, to the Zodiac—an enigma, a mystery, by itself.

Although that would suggest a much wider scope of the mechanism's functions, de Solla Price identified it as "a calendrical Sun and Moon computing mechanism which may have been made about 87 B.C."—a mechanism that "evolved as a result of Hipparchan modifications to the Archimedian planetarium." He considered it evidence "of the [higher] level of Greco-Roman mechanical proficiency than has been thought . . . a singular artifact that quite changes our ideas about the Greeks."

He thus remained true to the title of the book—"Gears from the **Greeks.**"

***

I found that these conclusions not only failed to answer the How, Why, and Who really designed and built this incredible device, but also lavished exuberant praise on "the Greeks" for astronomical knowledge the credit for which belonged to Sumer via Babylon. I searched, in vain, for the words Sumer/Sumerian in the book; I did find one brief reference to "Babylonian astronomy":

> The mechanism displays the cyclical sequence of sets of discrete phenomena rather than a continuum of events in a flowing time. In this way it is perhaps more in the spirit of Babylonian astronomy and the modern digital computer than in that of the Greek geometrical models.

American Friends Of The Haifa Maritime Museum, Inc.
18 East 74th Street, P.O. Box 616, New York, N.Y. 10021, (212) ~-4509

March 22, 1982

Dear Sir/Madam:

   We are delighted to announce that Professor Derek J. de Solla Price of Yale University will be our guest speaker on Monday April 5, 1982, 7:30 P.M. at the Harvard Club of New York City, 27 West 44th Street. The subject of his lecture is:

   Is Computer Genius a Throwback To Ancient Babylonian Thought Styles?

   Dr. Price is Avalon Professor of the History of Science, Yale University. He is a renown authority in the field of physics and particularly in the field of history of science with special reference to the evolution of scientific instruments.

   You and your friends will be most welcome at the meeting, and we look forward to seeing you.

                              Sincerely yours,

                              J. Berlau

                              Dr. A. Joseph Berlau
                              Secretary

The favor of a reply is requested.
R.S.V.P. Dr. A. Joseph Berlau, Secretary
(   ) 761-5299

Figure 109

Finding this small bow to Mesopotamia, I sent Prof. Price a copy of *The 12th Planet* with a letter pointing out the Sumerian origins of the Zodiac, etc. I did not receive an answer, but a year or so later—in March 1982—I was invited to attend a lecture by him at the Harvard Club in New York. The subject of the lecture—***Is Computer Genius a Throwback to Ancient Babylonian Thought Styles?***—seemed to be in line with questions that I had posed to him.

The invitation (fig. 109) came from a society called American Friends of the Haifa Maritime Museum (an interesting and fascinating museum, a visit to which I highly recommend), and I of course attended. I came armed with photocopies of illustrations from my book, showing Mesopotamian artifacts which proved the Sumerian origins of the "ancient Babylonian"—and thus of Greek—astronomical knowledge.

The lecture was not accompanied by any slides or other depictional material. In line with previous lectures and essays by him (that had been available in print), he expounded on his theme that the Babylonians were wedded to a dull arithmetic while the Greeks took off with fanciful geometry. It was all in all rather academic, dwelling on scientific "thought styles" or philosophies that led in time to the computer age. There was no mention of Sumer or the Sumerians.

The Q&A part that followed was very brief, because the meeting also had to deal with the Society's board elections, etc., and my raised hand was ignored. All I managed was to say "hello" to Dr. Price after the lecture, before he left, and remind him of my letter and book; he said Yes, Hello, and turned to talk to the others who surrounded him. I wondered whether he really recalled who I was.

Prof. Derek de Solla Price passed away the next year, and my avenue of further contacts with him thus came to an abrupt end. Thanks, however, to two devoted fans of mine in England, one (Keith H.) a professional horologist and the other (Martin B.) a part-time one, I was kept abreast of important subsequent researches on the Mechanism—researches which only deepened the mystery, for they showed (among other things) that what Dr. Price considered to be just two "sandwich" groups of moving parts were in fact *seventeen* layers of gears (fig. 110)!

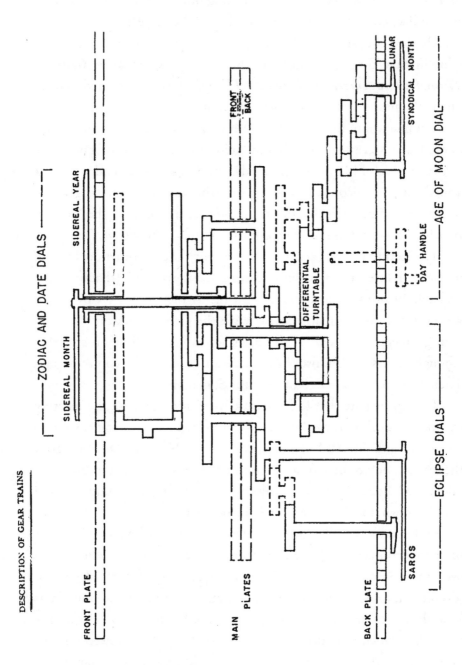

Figure 110

The first important study was an "analysis through reconstruction" by Alan G. Bromley, a computer scientist at the University of Sydney in Australia, in collaboration with a renowned Australian clockmaker, Frank Percival. Their detailed report in the *Horological Journal* of July 1990 related their unending difficulties in duplicating the gears and their precise teeth, in attaching this part to that part, in fitting it all within the tiny spaces, and in trying to make it work. They kept failing in cutting teeth at 60°. All along, they "wondered how the ancients did it." How, for example, do you divide a dial into 79 equal parts? How do you make contrate gears move in reverse?

Exasperated, Prof. Bromley wrote this in conclusion: "I do not pretend to have all the answers to how the Antikythera Mechanism was made, any more than I pretend to complete knowledge of its function or the mathematics of its gear work . . . The only inescapable fact is that, however it was done, the Antikythera Mechanism was made by craftsmen over 2,000 years ago."

The most thorough subsequent effort was by M. T. Wright, Curator of Mechanical Engineering at the Science Museum in London, who has labored over the Mechanism for many years. Not relying on Price's study of the Mechanism's fragments, he re-studied it with the latest technologies, even bringing over to Greece a huge apparatus for Linear Tomography. He then attempted to fathom the Mechanism's secrets by building an accurate duplicate thereof.

The resulting research paper, published in the *Horological Journal* in May 2002, disagreed with Price in various technical points, suggested that some parts were still missing, and concluded that the Mechanism was an Orrery—a mechanical model of the solar system that shows the orbits of the planets around the Sun in the correct relative velocities. Yet, though the study dwelled a lot on the *zodiacal aspects* of the device, it offered no explanation for the obvious paradox: Why do you need a complex *zodiacal* mechanism to show how Venus or Jupiter—which are planets—orbit around the Sun? And what was the purpose of the Mechanism's elaborate Moon/Sun relationships (which underlie *eclipse* phenomena)?

***

The fact that even the substantial researches conducted by Bromley, Percival, and Wright left key questions unanswered, led a group of British and Greek scientists, with the help of American computer and imaging experts, to launch, under the aegis of the National Bank of Greece, *The Antikythera Mechanism Research Project*. Using even more advanced techniques, and testing the results by constructing an updated model of the Mechanism, they presented their findings at an international conference held in Athens, Greece, November 30–December 1, 2006. Their full report was published in the November 30, 2006, issue of the journal *Nature*.

By combing the Athens Museum's stores of artifacts from the sunken ship and with the aid of CT-tomography, this latest team found a few more tiny fragments of the mechanism, established that there were at least 30 gears, probably 32, and perhaps as many as 37—some of them truly miniature. They were also able to read additional letters on the wooden or metal parts, and disclosed that some of the letters were a microscopical 2 millimeters (0.08 inches) in size.

As baffling as these findings were, the most astounding discovery of technological sophistication was that two connected gear-wheels were purposely slightly misaligned, with an ingenious pin from one gear moving the other gear back and forth to simulate the irregular elliptical orbit of the Moon around the Earth. That, the scientists pointed out, was essential if the purpose was to be able **to *predict* lunar and solar eclipses.** "When you see that, your jaw just drops and you think 'bloody hell, that's clever—that's brilliant technical design,'" said astronomy professor Michael Edmunds, a team leader from the University of Cardiff in Wales.

When it came to the question of *Who had such technology* centuries B.C., the team's best guess stayed with the Hipparchus/Rhodes island suggestions, although they repeatedly stressed that there has not been found anything like it from either before or after times; the only much simpler geared mechanisms appeared in Europe more than a thousand years later. As to *Who had the astronomical knowledge* required for devising the Mechanism, they recognized—though without elaborating—the *"Babylonian legacy."* As to *Who needed such a mechanism and what for,* Prof. Edmunds simply said: We don't know. But another team member's answer was: "This would have been important for timing agricultural and religious festivals."

One is as amazed by such a ridiculous answer as much as one is amazed by the incredible technological, scientific, and astronomical aspects of the Mechanism; its existence in its time frame is as astounding as if one were told that Jesus communicated with his disciples by cell phone . . .

As the reader will find out by the end of this book, it was not until I completed my research for the *The End of Days* (the concluding volume of *The Earth Chronicles*) that **the portentous secret of the *Antikythera Predictor* dawned on me.**

12

NAZCA:
WHERE THE GODS
LEFT EARTH

n 1997 I was leading one of the Earth Chronicles Expeditions to Turkey, and I insisted—over the objections of the tour operator—that we go to the country's eastern part. The local people were concerned about the security situation, because violent clashes were taking place there between the Turkish army and Kurdish rebels. But I insisted on going there—to see and be in **Harran.** It was a journey intended to complete a circuit that began almost a decade earlier on the other side of the world.

Harran, in case the reader has missed Bible classes, is where Abraham's God-ordained journey to Canaan began, more than four thousand years ago. He came to Harran with his father and other family members from Ur, the Sumerian capital in southern Mesopotamia. It was in Harran that Rebecca was chosen to become the bride of Abraham's son Isaac, and where Isaac's son Jacob met and fell in love with Rachel. All three Hebrew patriarchs and their wives, and thus all their descendants—myself included—have an ancestral "umbilical cord" to Harran.

But that was not the only reason for wanting to go there. *The principal reason was to visit the remains of an ancient temple whose god took off and left the Earth—only to return fifty-five years later; a god who followed the skymap's route!*

Nowadays Harran is a sleepy town, surrounded by the remains of an impressive but crumbling defensive wall from Islamic and medieval times (plate 34), built when some crucial battles were fought there; its few inhabitants live in adobe houses shaped like beehives, to provide some coolness in the summer heat. But in ancient times Harran was a thriving commercial center, famed for its temple to the god Sin (the "Moon god," whose principal temple was in Ur), and for its scribal academies. Outside the town the well where Jacob met Rachel—so local traditions hold—is still there, now protected by a raised concrete platform (plate 35), with sheep flocks still grazing in the nearby meadows.

Within the walls a mound, where the ancient temple was, dominates the landscape (plate 36). It was there that archaeologists found four inscribed stelas that record eyewitness reports of the divine departure and return.

Two of the stelas were emplaced by the high priestess of the temple whose name was Adda-Gupi, and record the events as told by her. The other two belonged to her son Nabuna'id (plate 37 and fig. 111), and record how he was fated to become the last king of Babylon. It was in a year equivalent to 610 B.C., Adda-Gupi wrote, that the god Sin "got angry with the people and went up to heaven"; it was in 555 B.C. that, relenting (and given a promise to be restored to primacy in Ur itself), he returned. The return was an event the likes of which were legendary already in his days, Nabuna'id wrote on his stelas—

> This is the great miracle of Sin
> that has by gods and goddesses
> not happened to the Earth—
> since days of old unknown;
> That the people of the Earth
> had neither seen nor found written
> on tablets since days of old:
> That Sin, lord of gods and goddesses,
> residing in the heavens,
> has come down from the heavens—
> in full view of Nabuna'id, king of Babylon.

Figure 111

The full story is told in greater detail in *The End of Days,* the seventh book of *The Earth Chronicles* series, in which a mass of other evidence is provided to conclude that not only Sin (with his spouse and chamberlain) had left; with some exceptions, **it was a wholesale departure of the Anunnaki from Earth.**

Indeed, the departure was so comprehensive that even in Jerusalem, according to the Bible (Ezekiel 8:12), it was lamented that "Yahweh sees us no more—Yahweh has left the Earth!"

In the previous volumes of *The Earth Chronicles* and earlier in this book, the story has been told of the Anunnaki's coming to Earth from Nibiru, in need of gold to save their planet's dwindling (or damaged) atmosphere, and of the first "cities of the gods" established in the E.DIN—"Eden" in pre-Diluvial Mesopotamia—with a Mission Control Center, a Spaceport, Beacon Cities, and a Landing Corridor for their spacecraft and shuttlecraft. All that was wiped out by the Deluge, and was replaced by a similar layout in the Lands of the Bible—a Spaceport in the Sinai peninsula, in whose central plain the ground was firm, flat, and suitable for landings and takeoffs; a Mission Control Center in the future Jerusalem; the great pyramid and its companions in Giza as Guidance Beacons; and the pre-Diluvial Landing Place in the Lebanon Mountains ("Baalbek") as a shuttle base.

These four space-related sites (see fig. 16, page 20) were to play a key role in the affairs of gods and men not only in antiquity, but also in the present and even in the future. In *The Wars of Gods and Men* I described the Pyramid Wars (when the Great Pyramid was stripped of its functioning equipment), and the Nuclear Attack of 2024 B.C., when the Spaceport in the Sinai, and Sodom and Gomorrah, were obliterated. The obvious question, then, was this: ***Where was an alternative post-nuclear space facility from which the Anunnaki could leave?***

For the answer we have to look to South America; and when one goes there, the most amazing ancient remains are encountered.

***

The Deluge, the great Flood, that "swept over the Earth" some 13,000 years ago, destroyed not only all in the Edin, but also the vital gold-mining operations of the Anunnaki in southeastern Africa. But the same calamity that in one swoop deprived the Anunnaki of the gold in one location opened up for them an even better source in another location—in the Andes mountains of South America.

Sweeping over vast mother lodes of gold in what is now Peru and Bolivia, the avalanche of water exposed immense quantities of gold that needed neither mining nor smelting and refining: Nuggets of pure gold just lay there, to be found and retrieved in a method called Placer Mining—the way gold was first recovered millennia later in North America, when some 30,000 gold seekers swarmed into the mountains of Canada's Yukon Territory to pan for gold at the Klondike River.

The Anunnaki established their new gold center at a site near the shores of a great lake—the largest navigable body of freshwater at the highest elevation (some 13,000 feet) in the world—*Lake Titicaca* (fig. 112). Called *Tiahuanacu* (lately spelled *Tiwanaku*) by the area's Aymara natives, it was deemed by the Incas of Peru to be the place where the great god of ancient South America, *Viracocha,* placed the first humans, gave them a golden wand with which to locate the future Cuzco, and granted civilization to the forerunners of the Incas. Then he left and was gone from the Earth.

The first European explorer of Tiahuanacu in modern times, Ephraim George Squier (*The Primeval Monuments of Peru,* 1853) was

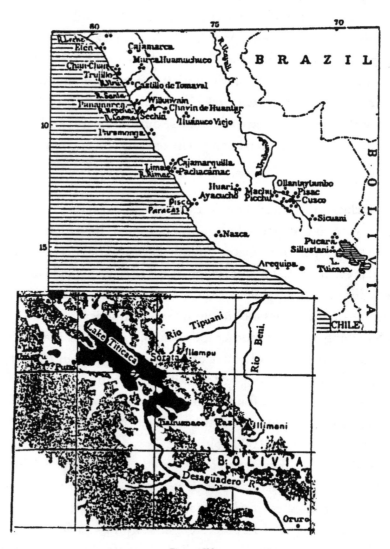

Figure 112

amazed to find in the windswept and barren place, at an elevation of almost four kilometers, the remains of monumental stone structures, large carved monoliths, statues representing giantlike unusual male beings, long conduits, subterranean tunnels. Why, he wondered, would *anyone* haul heavy stone boulders, erect immense buildings, or carve all that, in such a forbidding and almost lifeless place?

His amazement increased as he went the short distance to the lake's shore, where the ground was strewn with puzzling stone ruins. Finding a promontory, he gazed around and realized that the Lake and Tiahuanacu lay in a topographic depression, a once flat valley astride peaks that rose more than another 10,000 feet around it. Dominating the panorama were two grand peaks—Illampu and Illimani, rising to 27,000 and 25,000 feet, respectively (the highest in the Andes).

He could only think of the comparable twin peaks of Ararat, the highest in the Near East (though rising only to 17,000 and 13,000 feet), and he titled the chapter describing Tiahuanacu and its environs "Tiahuanacu, the Baalbec of the New World." Little did he realize how close he had come to a secret truth.

When I went to Tiahuanacu and Lake Titicaca in 1989, my primary "guidebook" was not one of the variety of tourists' handbooks then available, but heavier yellowing volumes of the writings of *Arthur Posnansky,* a European engineer who moved to Bolivia and devoted a lifetime to unraveling the enigmas of these ruins. The Spanish chronicler Pedro de Cieza de Leon, who traveled in Peru and Bolivia in 1532–1550, reported that "without doubt the ruins of Tiahuanacu were the most ancient place of any" that he had seen in those lands. *Arthur Posnansky astounded the scientific community by announcing, in his extensive writings beginning in 1914, that Tiahuanacu was built 12,000 years ago.*

The principal aboveground structures in Tiahuanacu (there are numerous subterranean ones) are the *Akapana,* an artificial hill riddled with channels, conduits, and sluices (in *The Lost Realms* I have suggested that it served as a metallurgical facility) and (apart from an enigmatic carved stone giant) a stone gateway known as the *Gate of the*

Sun (fig. 113)—a prominent structure that was cut and fashioned *from a single boulder.*

The main interest in the "Gate of the Sun" are the images carved on it, suggesting that it served a calendrical purpose, as the arrangement of the carved images on the archway indicates, and probably also a more sophisticated astronomical/zodiacal function. Those carvings are dominated by the larger central image of the god Viracocha (fig. 114) holding a forked lightning rod as his symbol, dominating a row of eleven smaller similar images (making twelve in all), and flanked by 30 "emissaries," fifteen on each side (fig. 115a, b) (adding up to days in a month).

Figure 113

Figure 114

a

b

Figure 115

These carvings served me as telltale clues, for they clearly emulated stone carvings that I had seen in Anatolia, in Hittite ruins, which represented the god Teshub (fig. 116) and his angelic emissaries (fig. 117a)—with obvious similarities of the Gate of the Sun images (fig. 117b) to the Hittite ones. He was, I wrote in *The Lost Realms,* the god Ishkur/Adad, Enlil's youngest son, known to the Hittite as Teshub ("The god of Storms"); and it was he who was sent to set up the new metallurgical center after the Deluge, bringing along from Anatolia some of his metallurgical experts.

Figure 116

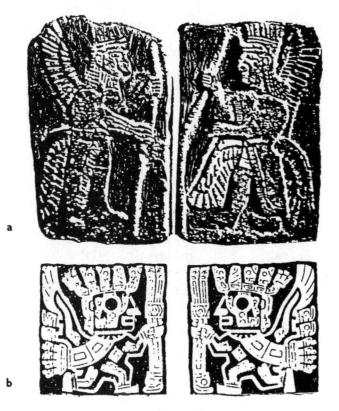

Figure 117

That he was there, in that part of South America, is witnessed by his symbol, left to see by all who approach (by sea or air). It is a huge depiction of a forked lightning, enigmatically carved on a steep mountainside (plate 38 and fig. 118) in the Bay of Paracas on Peru's coast northwest of Tiahuanacu; and it can be seen only from the air or from out in the Pacific Ocean. Nicknamed the Candelabra, the symbol is 420 feet long and 240 feet wide, and its lines, that are 5 to 15 feet wide, have been etched into the hard rocks to a depth of about two feet—and no one knows by whom and when or how, unless it was Adad himself who wanted to declare his presence . . .

The Gate of the Sun, where Adad/Teshub's image is the dominant feature, is so positioned that it forms an astronomical observation unit with the third prominent structure at Tiahuanacu, called the ***Kalasasaya.*** It is

Figure 118

a large rectangular structure, with a sunken central courtyard (fig. 119a), and is surrounded by standing stone pillars. Posnansky's suggestion that the Kalasasaya served as an observatory has been confirmed by subsequent explorers; his conclusion, based on Sir Norman Lockyer's archaeoastronomy guidelines, that the astronomical alignments of the Kalasasaya (fig. 119b) show that it was built thousands of years before the Incas was so incredible that German astronomical institutions sent teams of scientists to check this out. Their reports, and subsequent additional verifications, affirmed that the ***Kalasasaya's orientation unquestionably matched the Earth's obliquity either in 10000 B.C. or 4000 B.C.***

While the mixed (*incredulous* might be a better word) reception for those dates has not changed, as far as I have been concerned either one of the dates makes sense. The earlier date would synchronize well with my

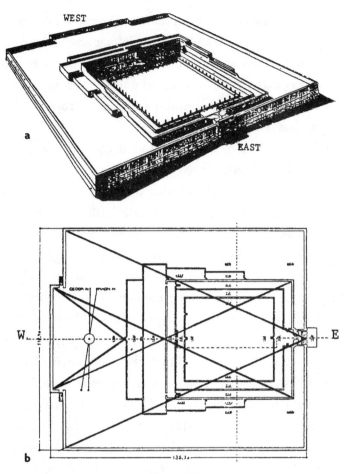

Figure 119

conclusions that Tiahuanacu was the new gold center of the Anunnaki after the Deluge (which I have dated to circa 11000 B.C.). The later date fits the time given by me for the state visit to Earth by Nibiru's ruler **Anu** and his spouse **Antu**—*a visit that offers the only explanation for the even more amazing remains at the nearby site called Puma Punku.*

***

Puma Punku is an odd place. Seemingly situated in the middle of nowhere, it is strewn with stone blocks of varied sizes, some gigantic, some small, some cut in most puzzling shapes (plate 39). They lie about scattered or in heaps, without apparent rhyme or reason. There are no standing structures that catch the eye, as in the nearby Tiahuanacu. "There is nothing to see there," tour guides say—as mine did—as they refuse to waste time to take sightseers there. But I insisted on going—as readers of *The Lost Realms* have also done later on; and it is a detour from the customary tourist circuit that is most worthwhile.

Posnansky's conclusions after some four decades of research also concerned Lake Titicaca itself; it used to be, he wrote, much larger with a water level some one hundred feet higher. So Puma Punku, now some distance from the current lakeshore, was actually built at the waters' edge, at the lake's southern shore, with harbor facilities. Its main remains consist of a row of four collapsed structures, ***each made of a single hollowed-out giant boulder*** (fig. 120). How such chambers were so precisely hollowed out of the gigantic stones, with ***inner corners*** and other baffling features precisely cut out (plate 40), or how four huge boulders were brought to the site, and why this was done, no archaeologist has yet figured out.

What is even more mind-boggling is the undisputable fact that each such hollowed-out set of chambers was ***completely inlaid inside with gold plates,*** held in place by gold nails accurately inserted in precise straight grooves (plate 41) incredibly cut into the hard stone surfaces. When the Spaniards arrived at the site in the sixteenth century, the mystery did not prevent them from prying loose the gold plates, and even extracting the golden nails, and hauling off an immense quantity of gold; it was all described by the Spanish chroniclers at the time, and rendered in greater detail in *The Lost Realms*.

There is yet another mystery at the site. The archaeological finds in the place included a large number of unusual stone blocks of varying sizes that were precisely cut, grooved, angled, and shaped; their complexity can best be described by showing some of them (from an 1892 report by the German archaeologists A. Stübel and Max Uhle, fig. 121). Though stone remnants, both from Puma Punku and from Tiahuanacu, have been constantly hauled away (mostly for use in local construction), many of the unbelievably complex cut stones still lie about in Puma Punku (plates 42, 43). One does not need an engineering degree to

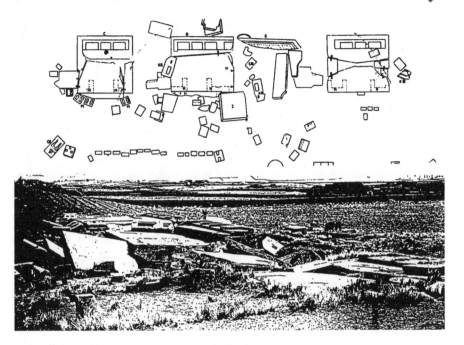

Figure 120

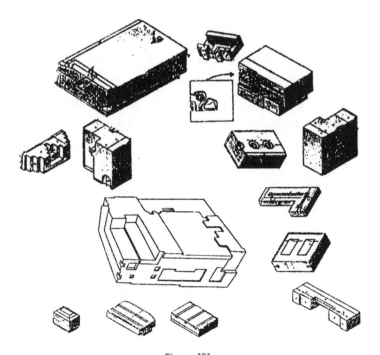

Figure 121

realize that these stones were cut, drilled, and shaped by someone with incredible technological ability and sophisticated equipment; indeed, one would doubt whether hard stones could be so shaped nowadays without shattering.

The puzzle is compounded by the mystery of what purpose did these technological miracles serve; obviously, for some unknown yet highly sophisticated purpose. If it was to serve as casting dies for complex instruments, what—and whose—were those instruments? Or were these elaborate stones themselves the instruments—components in even more complex equipment?

Of all the enigmas and mysteries on the southern shores of Lake Titicaca, the easiest for me to explain are the baffling gold-plated walls in the four-chamber structural unit. A similar golden enclosure exists, to this day in the Inca capital Cuzco—it is the *Coricancha,* the Holy of Holies in the main temple to Viracocha; and the term literally means "golden enclosure." (There too the visitor can see only the bare walls with the holes where the golden nails had been—the Spanish Conquistadores stripped it all there also.) A similar golden enclosure existed in *Jerusalem*—there too it was the Holy of Holies in the temple that King Solomon built, circa 950 B.C. And all of them emulated the gold-enclosed chambers in Uruk, back in Mesopotamia, where Anu and Antu had stayed during their state visit to Earth circa 4000 B.C.

The "golden enclosures" in Puma Punku, I have suggested, were constructed for the same purpose—as guest houses for Nibiru's ruler and his spouse when they came from Uruk to visit the gold-producing center on the shores of the Andean lake.

***

In 4000 B.C. the spaceport in the Sinai peninsula was still intact, available to be used by Anu and Antu for their space journeys from and to Nibiru. Not so in the crucial time slot 610–555 B.C., for that spaceport was destroyed, with nuclear weapons, back in 2024 B.C. The resulting question is obvious: Where was the Anunnaki's space facility in the intervening millennium and a half?

They still had the Landing Place in the Lebanon Mountains. It might have been good enough for shuttlecraft, but whether good enough to reach the Way Station on Mars, or a substitute spaceport on Earth, one cannot say for sure. The great powers of the second and first millenniums B.C. fought for control of this Landing Place. The Canaanite called it the Crest of Secrets, and detailed in their "myths" how the god Ba'al ("Lord") instructed the Divine Craftsman to refurbish its instruments. Later, the Phoenicians depicted it on their coins—platform and ready-to-launch rocketship included (fig. 122). And finally the Prophet Ezekiel, exiled to the nearby area of Harran, saw the famed Celestial Chariot—circa the fateful date of 555 B.C.

As far as the god Sin was concerned, having departed from Harran, he could have well used that close-by Landing Place. He apparently went just to Mars and not all the way to Nibiru, for he was back in half a century. But what and where was a major spaceport like the Sinai's had been, with long stretches of hard and flat terrain, for use by long-distance spacecraft? What about a facility not too far from the sources of the gold that had to be hauled all the way back to Nibiru—a facility that could then be used for the Grand Departure, if all the Anunnaki, leaders and rank and file, with all their varied craft and equipment and other belongings, were taking off—along, one must assume, with the last cargo of gold?

Figure 122

I now know where the place was. I had been there in 1994. But I did not realize what it really was until my later researches reached the crucial events of the Divine Departure. Thousands of others have also been there. It is known as the *pampa,* the treeless plain, of the **Nazca Lines.**

***

The **Nazca Lines,** called by some "the world's largest artworks," are located in a desert area between the Ingenio and Nazca Rivers in southern Peru. They represent, without doubt, one of the most puzzling riddles of antiquity.

In a vast *pampa* area (some 200 square miles!) that extends eastward from the Pacific Ocean to the rugged Andes mountains, in the direction of Lake Titicaca, "someone" used the ground as a canvas to draw on it scores of images; the drawings are so huge that they make no sense at ground level—but when viewed from the air, they clearly depict known and imaginary animals and birds (fig. 123, plates 44, 45). The "drawings" were made by removing the topsoil to a depth of several inches, and were executed with a unicursal line—one continuous line that curves and twists without crossing over itself. Various attempts to show that a horde of workers working at ground level and using scrapers could have created these images, have dismally failed. But anyone flying over the area invariably concludes that "someone" *airborne* had used a soil-blasting device to doodle on the ground below.

Who was there in ancient times with such capabilities—airborne and equipped with some ray gun gizmo? Those who scoff at the "Extraterrestrials" suggestion have tried both "natives airborne in primitive balloons" or "natives scraping the ground inch by inch" as solutions—only to end up even more ridiculed than Ancient Astronauts proponents. Though etched only inches deep rather than the feet-deep carving of the "Candelabra" in nearby Bay of Paracas, it was probably attained the same way. Indeed, as part of the answer to both enigmas, I included in my Briefing Notes to my Earth Chronicles Expedition group going to Nazca illustrations from other ancient sites in the Americas of ray guns in use (as this one from Tollan, Mexico in fig. 124); it is carved upon

ft 600 500 400 300 200 100 0

Figure 123

Figure 124

stone columns alongside giant carvings of strange warriorlike beings—the locals nicknamed them *Atlantes*—each equipped with exactly such a ray gun (fig. 125).

We are looking at the handiwork of the Anunnaki, I told my group without hesitation.

The doodles—some researchers give them a scientific-sounding name, "geoglyphs"—are far from being the only riddle of Nazca. Another and even more puzzling feature of the Nazca Lines are *actual "lines"* that run straight without fault. These plane stretches—sometimes narrow, sometimes wide, sometimes short, sometimes long—run over hills and vales, no matter the shape of the terrain (fig. 126, plate 46). There are some 740 such straight "lines," sometimes combined with triangular "trapezoids" (fig. 127). They frequently crisscross each other without rhyme or reason, sometimes running over and ignoring the animal drawings. What are they, who made them, how? These ones were clearly not made with handheld ray guns . . .

Various attempts to resolve the mystery of the Lines, including those by the late Maria Reiche who settled there and made the Lines her lifelong project, failed whenever an explanation was sought in terms of "it was done by native Peruvians"—people of a presumed "Nazca culture" or a purported "Paracas civilization" or the likes. Studies (including by the National Geographic Society) aimed at uncovering astronomical orientations for the Lines—alignments with solstices, equinoxes, this or that star—led nowhere. For those who rule out an "Ancient Astronauts" solution, the enigma remains unresolved.

Though the wider lines look like airport runways, on which wheeled aircraft roll to take off (or to land), this is not the case here, if only because the "lines" are not horizontally level—they run straight over uneven terrain, ignoring hills, ravines, gullies. They are not "runways" as we understand the term. Indeed, having looked at countless photographs and having been there and flown over the Lines back and forth, it seemed to me that rather than being there to *enable* takeoff, they are the *result of takeoffs* by **craft taking off and leaving on the ground below "lines" created by their engine's exhaust.** That the "celestial

Figure 125

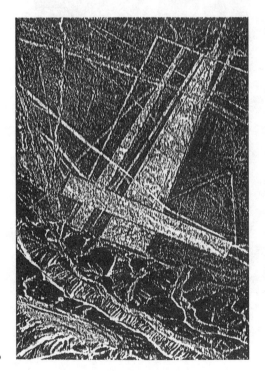

Figure 126

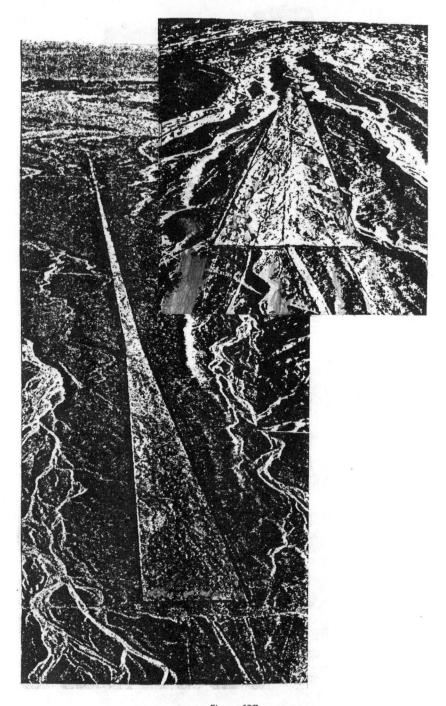

Figure 127

chambers" of the Anunnaki did emit such exhausts is indicated by the Sumerian pictograph DIN.GIR for the spaceborne gods (fig. 128), or a visual depiction on a cylinder seal of a rocketship seen in the skies of the island of Crete (fig. 129).

***

Did ancient-astronaut pilots use the Nazca flatland as their final space-port, doodling for fun while killing time before takeoffs?

All I can say for sure is that the suggestion that ancient pilots were involved in the Nazca Lines' enigmas is supported by yet another inexplicable mystery in that part of Peru. I became aware of it through a report, by a member of the Ancient Astronaut Society, writing in the Society's news-letter *Ancient Skies*. She reported an intriguing landmark not far from the Nazca Lines; responding to my request, she sent me a photograph.

When I and my Expeditions group went to see Nazca, we stopped at a certain spot on the Pan American Highway where an observation tower enabled visitors to take a better-than-flat look at the nearby doodles; that, of course, was not enough. We stayed at a hotel in the nearest town (Ica), and drove in the morning to a small airfield (actually, one short runway) where tiny four-seat planes were available to take tourists sightseeing from the air. The flights followed a set pattern, with the pilot acting as a guide, circling over the "giant" or the "monkey" doodles long enough for picture taking; then a run over some of the Lines, and back to the airstrip.

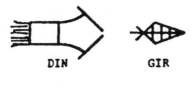

DIN   GIR

Figure 128

Figure 129

With only three passengers per flight, our group needed several such flights by two alternating aircraft. Thus getting acquainted with the pilots, I pulled out the intriguing photograph, and asked what they knew about this feature. They knew nothing. Maybe Carlos would know, one said. Carlos was a third pilot who had yet to show up in the relief team. There was an "Aeroporto" shack near the airstrip, serving cold beverages and selling souvenirs. We have to wait, I told my group.

In time, Carlos showed up. I showed him the photograph. Yes, he said, I heard of this place. Do you know where it is? I asked. I think so, he said; I know the direction. Can you take me there? I asked. We'll have to circle there and look for it, he warned me.

Financial negotiations with him and with the pilot who was to be relieved followed. When the price was agreed upon—paid in advance in U.S. dollars—I asked one of my group, Frederick "Fritz" Meyer, to accompany me. He was a veteran pilot with United Airlines, flying on international routes to varied airports with the oddest landing patterns. He readily agreed to come along.

The flight, lasting almost half an hour, took us away from the flat pampa into the rugged mountains—in a southwesterly direction, as I recall. The pilot flew about here and there, turning, going higher and lower. We won't find it, I thought to myself. And then—*there it was!*

Incredibly, in the middle of nowhere, there were clear and unmistakable markings of circles and squares forming a cross—as in a modern heliport!

Adhering to the saying that a picture is worth a thousand words, here is what we saw (plates 47, 48).

My companion Fritz, the experienced airlines pilot, saw much more in the complex designs and their precise details. He thought that the whole design of concentric circles, rectangles, triangles, and dots was not just "a directional indicator to a certain place," but also an identifier and provider of information through the placement of the "dots." If they were modern "points of light," their switching on and off to create varied patterns could provide a pilot with a wealth of information.

But these are not modern points of light, and the only "air facility" within miles are the Nazca Lines . . . Could the local pilots explain it? No. Is it marked on *any* airmap? No. It is an enigma that is yet to be resolved, a mystery yet to be explained. But that it is part of the greater Nazca Lines mystery, of that I have no doubt.

For all this—Lines, doodles, heliport-like markings—there is one single plausible solution: Nazca was the last spaceport of the Anunnaki. It served them after the one in the Sinai was destroyed—and then it served them for the Final Departure.

POSTSCRIPT:
PROPHECIES OF THE RETURN

T he inevitable conclusion from all that must be that, from at least 610 B.C. through probably 560 B.C., the Anunnaki gods were methodically leaving planet Earth," I wrote in *The End of Days,* the concluding volume of *The Earth Chronicles* series. Its subtitle is *Armageddon and Prophecies of the Return;* and as stated in a previous chapter, it was only when I had arrived at those conclusions that the enigmatic fog enveloping the Antikythera Mechanism began to lift.

The *Day of the Lord* of biblical prophecies, I concluded in *The End of Days,* was a day when a solar eclipse was to occur; and was it just a coincidence that a principal purpose of the Mechanism was to *predict* lunar *and solar* eclipses?

One of the clearest markings in the Mechanism that may throw light on its time and purpose is a broken part with *gradations and a pointer,* accompanied by writing (fig. 130). Identifying the writing as month names, Dr. Price concluded that the Mechanism was designed to correct the Greek calendar of 365 days in a solar year to the correct 365.25 days (which we correct by adding a leap day every four years).

He concluded that the Pointer was emplaced so as to mark a very specific date. Could it be the date of some major event from which the Mechanism's count began?